That I May See

Journeying from Spiritual Confusion and
Blindness To the Radiance of the Eucharist

Fr. Barry Braum

ADORATIO
PRESS

Nihil Obstat: Reverend Monsignor Richard G. Henning, S.T.D.

Censor Librorum

October 23, 2017

Cover Photo by Josh Applegate

Cover design: Adoratio Press

ISBN-13: 978-0-9997093-1-3
ISBN-10: 0-9997093-1-3

Adoratio Press, Houston
www.adoratiopress.com

DEDICATION

To Our Lady, His Mother and mine.

CONTENTS

———————•———————

ACKNOWLEDGEMENTS

I am very grateful to all those who have helped in the preparation of this book:

My family, all the priests in my community, Bishop John Barres, Bishop Dominique Rey, Fr. Douglas Mosey, CSB, Monsignor Richard Henning, Fr. Paul Murray, OP, Fr. Anthony Mary, MFVA, Dr. Cynthia Toolin-Wilson, Tina Dennelly, Lucille Hess, Angela McMorrow, Carol Kassick, and all who have supported the work through their prayers.

FOREWORD

———————•———————

With a depth that comes from contemplating the Word of God in Scripture and in His Eucharistic presence, this approach to the new evangelization is truly a sign of a life lived in union with God. Written by one whose community's charism includes many hours of Eucharistic Adoration, it reveals the depths of a spirituality that is unveiled through meditative praying of the Scriptures. Father Braum is masterful in leading the reader through one story of Scripture, the story of the blind beggar of the Gospels, Bartimaeus. He tracks his journey from blindness to sight and from interior darkness to light. The journey is a paradigm for any and all. The map for the journey is built on five principles which the author claims were fixed in his heart during a retreat and which he later saw as foundation stones for the spiritual life. He writes a chapter on each principle: Sanctifying Grace, Marian Consecration, Eucharistic Adoration, Immersion in the Mysteries of Christ through the Gospels and the Rosary, and holy Communion. We can also see in them a summary of Pope St. John Paul II's pastoral plan for the new millennium. Bartimaeus looked into the face of Christ and begged to see. Father Braum in this book invites its readers also to look into the face of Christ, particularly in Eucharistic Adoration. With a wealth in precisely chosen footnotes, there is an abundance of material for prayerful reflection. At once scholarly and accessible, this work promises to be a meditation and inspiration for anyone whose longing heart yearns to be evangelized or to evangelize.

Very Rev. Douglas L. Mosey, C.S.B.

Rector of Holy Apostles College and Seminary

INTRODUCTION

———— • ————

In one of his retreats given to priests, Bishop Fulton
Sheen said that the greatest tragedy would be to come to
the end of our lives and realize that the "Lord was so
near, and yet we were so far away."[1] Our greatest regret
will be that Jesus had waited every day to see us, to grant
us grace, and to pour out blessings upon us, and yet we
had never gone to visit him. The whole purpose of our
lives is to fall in love with the Eucharist—which is to fall
in love with God. Saint Edith Stein put it beautifully
when she wrote: "It is most important that the holy
Eucharist becomes life's focal point: that the eucharistic

---

[1] Fulton Sheen, *The Eucharist God Among Us*, Retreat on the
Priesthood 2, 29 mins 36 secs Audio, from FultonSheen.com
(Catholic MP3 Vault, 2011).

Savior is the center of existence; that every day is received from his hand and laid back therein; that the day's happenings are deliberated with him. In this way, God is given the best opportunity to be heard in the heart, to form the soul, and to make its faculties clear-sighted and alert for the supernatural."[2]

J. R. R. Tolkien expresses deep regret at not emphasizing the Blessed Sacrament enough to his children. He wrote to his son saying, "But I fell in love with the Blessed Sacrament from the beginning—and by the mercy of God never have fallen out again: but alas! I indeed did not live up to it. I brought you all up ill and talked to you too little. Out of wickedness and sloth I almost ceased to practice my religion . . . Not for me the Hound of Heaven, but the never-ceasing silent appeal of Tabernacle, and the sense of starving hunger. I regret those days bitterly (and suffer for them with such patience as I can be given); most of all because I failed as a father. Now I pray for you all, unceasingly, that the Healer (the Hcelend as the Savior was usually called in

[2] Edith Stein, *Essays on Woman*, 2nd ed., ed. L. Gelber and Romaeus Leuven (Washington, D. C.: ICS Publications, 1996), Kindle edition, loc. 2049-2052.

Old English) shall heal my defects, and that none of you shall ever cease to cry *Benedictus qui venit in nomine Domini*."[3]

After several years of formation in religious life, I was home on vacation visiting my family in South Africa. This was prior to my entering major seminary and the last years of preparation for ordination to the holy priesthood. During this visit, I was blessed to spend some time with a dear priest friend of mine, a man who was greatly influential, primarily by his example, in my first ever wanting to be a priest. When I was discerning the call to the priesthood I had made a retreat at his parish. It was during that retreat that the Lord fixed five principles within my heart. At the time, they were simply the fondest memories and experiences of the retreat. It was only later that I began to see them as foundation stones for the spiritual life. These graces or principles are in essence simply the choice to anchor ourselves to the Eucharist through Mary, scripture, and the sacraments. Practically speaking, there are five principle ways to do this: confession, consecration to Mary, daily eucharistic

---

[3] J. R. R. Tolkien, *The Letters of J. R. R. Tolkien: A Selection*, ed. Humphrey Carpenter and Christopher Tolkien (HarperCollins Publishers), Kindle edition, loc. 7233-7239.

adoration, daily scriptural meditation with daily Rosary, and daily Mass and holy Communion. I don't believe I truly appreciated how important these principles were at the time, but I grow in gratitude for them with each passing day. Placing the Eucharist as one of the principles does not mean that the other principles are equal to the Eucharist in dignity and importance. The Eucharist sits above the other principles as God sits above his creation because the Eucharist is God himself. The other principles serve only to better unite us to the Lord, and are important only in so far as they mediate the graces of Christ to us. It is to highlight this Eucharistic supremacy that the Eucharist and Adoration make up the book's central chapter. As believers, all of us are called to live our lives for and from the Eucharist because then we will be living our lives for and from Jesus. These graces, these principles, were and are the building blocks we see in the lives of all the saints. They can be found in every single biography of every single saint. And yet, however obvious their necessity, they can easily be overlooked or forgotten. We don't spend our time thinking about sunlight, air, and water, and yet these are among our most natural and most essential needs.

At the time of the retreat, I was already going often to confession, praying the Rosary, and attending Mass regularly if not daily. I was also in eucharistic adoration frequently. However, the retreat made me realize the importance of consciously fixing these five principles into my daily and weekly life. The first grace, which came during the first day of the retreat—and the sweetest grace of my life—was that I fell in love with Our Lady. I immediately consecrated myself to her with all my heart. Interestingly, in a conversation with my dad shortly before making this retreat, I had told him that I was discerning a call to the priesthood. Having mentioned to him that I felt unworthy of the call and was afraid of failing in so noble a vocation, he responded directly: "You need a deep and loving relationship with Our Lady, and you don't have one yet; but Mary is essential for the faithful living out of any vocation." He had the wisdom of his own personal experience of coming to know and love Our Lady and was able to point out the hole in my spiritual life. He was absolutely right, and I am forever grateful for what he said. I prayed the Rosary daily, but Mary was just one of the other saints to me. I was as devoted to her as I was to Saint Pio. When I went back and asked my dad how to even begin a deeper relationship with Mary, he said simply, "Just ask her to take care of that." And so I did.

On that retreat, I received a particular and overwhelming grace of love and devotion to Mary; she completely changed for me from that point. I saw her from that moment on not as simply one among the many saints, but as the Mother of God and queen of heaven and earth. I experienced her not as someone distant and indifferent, but as an ever-present attentive mother. The experience was one that made clear to me her concern for every detail of my life. I came to know the love of God through Mary. I was completely saturated in the tender love of our heavenly mother. Little did I know that at that time, my own mother (who was visiting her family in Ireland), after hearing that I was making a retreat, began visiting all the local churches and lighting candles in front of each image of Our Lady, praying for the grace that I would fall in love with my heavenly mother. Her prayers were answered abundantly.

What immediately flowed from the consecration to Mary was a deeper sorrow for all the ways in which I had offended God in my life. Added to this was also a profoundly deeper love for the Mass and, consequently, a desire for more eucharistic adoration. ". . . Eucharistic adoration is simply the natural consequence of the eucharistic celebration. . . . The act of adoration outside Mass prolongs and intensifies all that takes place during the liturgical celebration itself."[4] I can see now that Mary was orienting my whole life toward her Son present in the Blessed Sacrament. Anyone who turns to Mary will be lead to the Eucharist because "the most holy Eucharist contains the Church's entire spiritual wealth: Christ himself, our passover and living bread."[5] Like any mother, Mary is concerned with our nourishment, growth, and safety. This is why Our Lady leads us to the heavenly food where we can be nourished, and she hides us in the shadow of his eucharistic wings where we are kept safe. Mary takes us by the hand and leads us to the source of life that is her Son, the Word, through whom all things were created and through whom all things are

---

[4] Pope Benedict XVI, Post-Synodal Apostolic Exhortation on the Eucharist as the Source and Summit of the Church's Life and Mission *Sacramentum Caritatis* (22 February 2007), § 66.

[5] Pope John Paul II, Encyclical on the Eucharist in its Relationship to the Church *Ecclesia de Eucharistia* (17 April 2003), § 1.

recreated. Her desire is that we will set the Eucharist at the center of our lives. "The Church was born of the paschal mystery. For this very reason the Eucharist, which is in an outstanding way the sacrament of the paschal mystery, *stands at the center of the Church's life.*"[6]

I witnessed many miracles of grace and healing during my time on retreat, and I received the confirmation of a call to become a priest myself, by God's grace and the intercession of Our Lady, who was dedicated to serving Christ in the Blessed Sacrament. I desired to live a life consecrated to Mary, governed by our eucharistic King, seeking daily inspiration and guidance at his feet in adoration.

Some years later, as a priest, at the seminary where I had been formed, I gave a conference on these five principles which center us on the Eucharist. Afterward, I was asked if it would be possible to write the conference in book format. This book will be an attempt to do that. It is by no means a comprehensive book on the spiritual life but rather a simple look at five practical principles that, if embraced with love, will unite us more intimately

---

[6] *Ecclesia de Eucharistia,* § 3.

to Jesus in the Eucharist, who is the source and summit, the Alpha and Omega, the beginning and the end. If the Eucharist is not the foundation upon which we build our lives, the means by which we build, and the goal toward which we build, it is evidence that we either do not yet fully understand, or are not fully convinced, of the doctrine of the Real Presence. "For no other foundation can anyone lay than that which is laid, which is Jesus Christ" (1 Cor 3:11).

Finding These Principles in the Life of Jesus

The retreat mentioned above was a moment in my life that could be likened to being healed from blindness. Not a physical blindness, obviously, but a more serious spiritual blindness. An interior dullness that meant I was blind to the greatest gift of God—the holy Eucharist. In Baptism we receive a participation in the life of God, and so it is the most necessary sacrament for us in order to be saved. In the Eucharist, however, we receive Jesus Christ himself: body, blood, soul, and divinity. In the Eucharist is contained God himself, and therefore there is no greater gift. "The Church has received the Eucharist from Christ her Lord not as one gift—however precious—

among so many others, but as *the gift par excellence*, for it is the gift of himself, of his person in his sacred humanity, as well as the gift of his saving work."[7] In the Eucharist, Jesus loves us to the extremes of love. ". . . When Jesus knew that his hour had come to depart out of this world to the Father, having loved his own who were in the world, he loved them to the end" (Jn 13:1). My experience on that retreat was like having scales fall from my eyes to reveal a love that had always been there, to what was right in front of me and freely available to all who ask, seek, and knock. Maybe that is the reason I have such a love for the healing of Bartimaeus. I suppose I am drawn back, again and again, to ponder his healing because it is the miracle in which I can see all the elements of my own ongoing conversion toward Jesus in the Blessed Sacrament.

---

[7] *Ecclesia de Eucharistia*, §11.

THE FIRST PRINCIPLE:
CONFESSION AND A RETURN TO
SANCTIFYING GRACE

———————— • ————————

And they came to Jericho; and as he was leaving Jericho . . .

(Mk 10:46).

In the tenth chapter of the Gospel of Mark, we find the scene from the life of Christ where Jesus heals the blind man named Bartimaeus. Interestingly, this miracle is the last miracle that Jesus worked before he entered into holy week. There are other miracles in the city, such as the withering of the fig tree, which he performs during the week leading up to his Passion; but this is the last miracle before Jesus's triumphant entry into Jerusalem.

Therefore, this last miracle is very significant due to its placement—a kind of "saving the best for last," if you will. There are so many details recounted in the scene, details that can teach us profound truths about the spiritual life if we take the time to ponder them in our hearts.

The Second Vatican Council emphasized that there is a universal call to holiness. "Therefore in the Church, everyone whether belonging to the hierarchy, or being cared for by it, is called to holiness, according to the saying of the Apostle: 'For this is the will of God, your sanctification.'"[8] So everyone is called to become deeply holy and thus deeply contemplative. Holiness is the coming of God's kingdom within us. It is the amount we allow Jesus to live in us until we can say with Saint Paul, "It is no longer I who live, but Christ who lives in me" (Gal 2:20). We are called to heaven, and the activity of heaven is the loving contemplation of God by the saints. We will see God as he is, and our whole being will be permeated with ecstatic joy. We can also only enter heaven as saints—so that life of grace, contemplation,

---

[8] Pope Paul VI, Dogmatic Constitution on the Church *Lumen Gentium* (21 November 1964), § 39.

and holiness has to begin now. It must grow in this life and, it is hoped, reach the perfection of *transforming union.*[9] We must always be living in grace, growing in holiness, and entering into the loving contemplation of God through meditation on the life of Christ and his mysteries. The only way to the Father is through the Son. We have to enter into a life of union with Jesus through his grace, his Mother, his word, and his presence in the holy Eucharist.

The Healing of Bartimaeus

As is true of all scripture, the miracle of the healing of Bartimaeus is a divinely revealed "roadmap" for entering more deeply into the life of holiness and prayer. In Bartimaeus we see a beautiful response to the call to perfection, to which we are all called by Christ, who said: "You, therefore, must be perfect, as your heavenly Father is perfect" (Mt 5:48). Perfection is the fulfillment of a lack. For something to be perfect means that it lacks nothing. Bartimaeus lacked sight in the beginning, but his eyes are made perfect and whole at the end. In a spiritual

---

[9] Transforming union or spiritual marriage is the height of the spiritual life, the union of a soul with God in deep contemplation.

sense he therefore moves from imperfection to perfection. The choice for perfection is essentially a death to ourselves. Although many will choose to leave an evil life for a good life in grace, there are few who choose to go from a good life to a life of perfection. "Many are called, but few are chosen" (Mt 22:14). The former is a choice to receive the graces of the Cross, the latter is a choice for the Cross itself. Let's look at Bartimaeus and imitate his response so that we can be healed and made perfect.

> *And they came to Jericho; and as he was leaving Jericho with his disciples and a great multitude, Bartimaeus, a blind beggar, the son of Timaeus, was sitting by the roadside. And when he heard that it was Jesus of Nazareth, he began to cry out and say, "Jesus, Son of David, have mercy on me!" And many rebuked him, telling him to be silent; but he cried out all the more, "Son of David, have mercy on me!" And Jesus stopped and said, "Call him." And they called the blind man, saying to him, "Take heart; rise, he is calling you." And throwing off his mantle he sprang up and came to Jesus. And Jesus said to him, "What do you want me to do for you?" And the blind man said to him, "Master, let me*

receive my sight." And Jesus said to him, "Go your way; your faith has made you well." And immediately he received his sight and followed him on the way (Mk 10:46-52).

"And they came to Jericho; and as he was leaving Jericho with his disciples and a great multitude . . ." The first line from this scene is very interesting. They come to Jericho, and then they leave. Why even mention Jericho? In Luke's Gospel we know that the Lord calls Zacchaeus, the man who climbed a tree in order to see Christ, to conversion in Jericho. Mark's account, however, makes no reference to anything that took place in that city. So why does he mention it? Why does he say it in this way specifically? I believe it is included because, in a mystical sense, it teaches us about the first necessary principle in our journey toward Christ. To arrive at the principle we must first look at the city of Jericho and then at the movement of Christ. Regarding Jericho, apart from being an actual city in the literal and historical sense, we can dig deeper into what Jericho represents both mystically and spiritually. It is an infamous city with a dark history. Once it had been destroyed, God had threatened severe punishments on anyone who sought to rebuild it.

Cursed before the Lord be the man that rises up and rebuilds this city, Jericho. At the cost of his first-born shall he lay its foundation, and at the cost of his youngest son shall he set up its gates (Jo 6:26).

Why such severe punishments for rebuilding a city? Well, it was the last stronghold against the Israelites when they had entered into the promised land; and so, in a sense, just as the promised land represents the kingdom of God, Jericho is a city that represents the kingdom of Satan and sin. Saint Jerome says that the name Jericho means "anathema," which is to be cut off from Christ and his Church.[10] Interpreted that way, the punishments for rebuilding Jericho are understandable, since the price paid by God the Father in the actual destruction of sin and death was his only begotten Son, the Beloved. Therefore what is seen here, with Jesus leaving Jericho and heading toward Jerusalem, is the mystery of salvation worked in and through Christ.

---

[10] Saint Jerome, "The name of the city agrees with the approaching Passion of Our Lord; for it is said, And they came to Jericho. Jericho means moon or anathema; but the failing of the flesh of Christ is the preparation of the heavenly Jerusalem." Thomas Aquinas, *Catena Aurea, Commentary on the Four Gospels*, vol. 1-4 (London, John Henry Parker: Oxford, 2011), Kindle Edition, loc. 20023-20024.

Anyone who has been to the Holy Land knows that the journey from Jericho to Jerusalem is an upward journey—each step toward Jerusalem is a step higher. And so the Lord is, in a certain sense, teaching us about the necessity to separate ourselves from the kingdom of sin and evil, and to move toward the kingdom of heaven that is prefigured by Jerusalem. And yet this necessary movement away from sin is beyond our individual power; we can only make it with Christ and by cooperation with his grace. That is why he leaves Jericho *with* his disciples and a great multitude. The multitude prefigures all those who will leave everything of the world and sin behind and follow Jesus in cooperation with his grace acting in them. We must leave behind Jericho, leave behind sin, and walk with Christ toward the heavenly Jerusalem. Anyone who is on the journey, or on the road of pursuing holiness, is on this walk with the Lord from Jericho to Jerusalem. It represents the necessary movement away from sin if we want to follow Christ. It also represents very vividly the growth in the spiritual life, which is a walk directed by Christ and strengthened by his grace.

Looking at the Old Testament and how the Lord destroys Jericho gives us valuable insight into how Jesus destroys sin and death in our own lives. We read the account of its destruction as follows:

> So he [Joshua] caused the ark of the Lord to compass the city, going about it once; and they came into the camp, and spent the night in the camp. Then Joshua rose early in the morning, and the priests took up the ark of the Lord. And the seven priests bearing the seven trumpets of rams' horns before the ark of the Lord passed on, blowing the trumpets continually; and the armed men went before them, and the rear guard came after the ark of the Lord, while the trumpets blew continually. And the second day they marched around the city once, and returned into the camp. So they did for six days. On the seventh day they rose early at the dawn of day, and marched around the city in the same manner seven times: it was only on that day that they marched around the city seven times. And at the seventh time, when the priests had blown the trumpets, Joshua said to the people, "Shout; for the Lord has given you the city. And the city and all that is within it shall be devoted to the Lord for destruction; only Rahab the harlot and all who are with her in her house shall live, because she hid the messengers that we sent. But you, keep yourselves from the things

devoted to destruction, lest when you have devoted them you take any of the devoted things and make the camp of Israel a thing for destruction, and bring trouble upon it. But all silver and gold, and vessels of bronze and iron, are sacred to the Lord; they shall go into the treasury of the Lord." So the people shouted, and the trumpets were blown. As soon as the people heard the sound of the trumpet, the people raised a great shout, and the wall fell down flat, so that the people went up into the city, every man straight before him, and they took the city (Jo 6:11-20).

The Lord gave very specific instructions detailing how to destroy Jericho. The success of the mission depended upon fidelity, on the part of Joshua and the Israelites, to the Word of God. Adam and Eve had rejected God's instruction, which caused death and suffering to enter the world. Therefore it is obedience to God's word that will overthrow sin and death. Christ was obedient unto death, and thus death was destroyed. The Israelites then, obedient to God's word and carrying out faithfully the actions God had instructed, caused the walls of Jericho to fall, and they could then destroy the city with fire. God's power, which destroyed the walls of

Jericho, was made dependent, by God's own will, on the Israelites performing all of the preceding actions exactly as God had willed them. This is in itself a powerful prefiguration of the sacraments of the Church and how the power of God's grace is bestowed and active through them.

First we have seven days, and on the seventh day an instruction to circle the city seven times. A reference to seven in scripture should always make us think of either creation, recreation, or the seven sacraments through which we are recreated. So the way in which Jericho is destroyed is a prefiguration of how sin is conquered in our lives through the seven sacraments. Firstly, just as God gave specific words and instruction to Joshua, we also have to take the words that Jesus gives us through the Church. These words then constitute the *form* of the sacraments. Secondly, in the same way that God instructed the priests to take the Ark of the Covenant and the rams' horns, we too must use the material or visible elements that Christ desires to be used. These visible elements then constitute the *matter* of the sacraments. Lastly, just as the Lord specifically instructs the priests to be the ones who carry the ark, we also have to use the instruments that Christ desires to work through for the administration of the sacraments. These chosen instruments then constitute the *ministers* of the sacraments.

In that light, then, the seventh day with seven processions is a reference to the highest of all the sacraments, i.e., the most Blessed Sacrament. Baptism is the first sacrament in order of time, but the Eucharist is the first sacrament in order of dignity because the Eucharist is Christ. The Blessed Sacrament is Jesus. The Blessed Sacrament is the consuming fire that burns away sin because it contains Christ himself. Under the humble appearance of bread and wine is the God of love! The Eucharist is the source of grace and the heart of the Church. "The Eucharist is 'the source and summit of the Christian life.' The other sacraments, and indeed all ecclesiastical ministries and works of the apostolate, are bound up with the Eucharist and are oriented toward it. For in the blessed Eucharist is contained the whole spiritual good of the Church, namely Christ himself, our Pasch."[11] All of our lives, all of our vocations, have to

---

[11] *Catechism of the Catholic Church*, revised ed. (London: Burns & Oates, 2011), 1324.

become centered on the Blessed Sacrament because only then are they truly centered on Jesus himself.

Those who are not destroyed when the Israelites attack are Rahab and all those who are united to her (or who "belong" to her, as the text says). She represents the Church, the people of God, the bride of Christ, who had gone astray in sin but had returned repentant. She was saved because she hid the messengers. This refers to the Church, who guards the prophets and Christ himself, who keeps the Old and New Testament and guards its integrity and correct interpretation. She is guardian of the messengers. Her household is also marked by a scarlet cord, representing the Precious Blood of Jesus, which is the price of our salvation. Another important detail is the instruction not to take anything from the city once it had been destroyed, besides those things that were reserved for God.

> *But you, keep yourselves from the things devoted to destruction, lest when you have devoted them you take any of the devoted things and make the camp of Israel a thing for destruction, and bring trouble upon it (Jo 6:18).*

This represents the roots or attachments to sin that linger within us even after sins are confessed and forgiven. If we don't pull out the roots, if we take anything back with us, it will end up drawing us back into sin and death. The Israelites longed for the fleshpots of Egypt while they wandered in the desert. This led them to develop a loathing for the manna from heaven, so the Lord permitted seraph serpents to plague the camp in order to teach the same principle of purification. Attachment to sin in our hearts will lead us back into sin unless it is uprooted.

Becoming Children of the Father

With all of those details, then, the first line in the healing of Bartimaeus takes on a whole new light. It communicates to us the necessity of moving away from sin, and we do this through the sacraments of Baptism and Reconciliation. "They came to Jericho, and as he was leaving Jericho . . ." *They* came, but *he* was leaving. The *they* represents us. We came to Jericho; we chose to sin and thus enter that city as slaves. But *he* is the One who conquers sin and leads us out from darkness, by means of the sacraments, into freedom as adopted children of our heavenly Father. Leaving Jericho means entering a state of grace through Baptism, or being restored to a state of grace through confession if we have fallen from grace through sin. Leaving behind sin through the sacrament of Reconciliation marks the beginning of our spiritual lives.

The spiritual life begins with grace. After a good examination of conscience we should ask ourselves if, to the best of our knowledge, we are in a state of grace. We need to look at the commandments and examine whether or not we have broken them in thought, word, or deed. If we have, then humbling ourselves before the triune God, we confess our sins and enter back into the life of the Trinity through the sacrament of Reconciliation. Sanctifying grace is our spiritual life. There isn't one without the other. Our spiritual life grows as sanctifying grace grows within us in intensity of love. If sanctifying grace is extinguished in us through mortal sin, the effects are mortal and we die spiritually. Generally we fear natural death more than spiritual death, yet spiritual death is infinitely more serious. We should fear mortal sin more than natural death, because if we die in grace we will enter eternal life due to the fact that eternal life is already begun within us. If, however, we die outside of grace, that state of death will go on for eternity. We cannot say we have a spiritual life if we are not in grace. We can have many spiritual practices, appear exteriorly as good people, feed the poor, help the sick, recite thousands of prayers, perform many kind deeds for others, preach the Gospel, and even attend Mass, but if I have not sanctifying grace, or love, as Saint Paul says, then I have nothing.[12] If we could be saved by our own good actions or numerous prayers, then Christ died in vain. Any good action only becomes meritorious when it is done in grace. "First of all there is nothing great in God's sight except that which is done for his glory, through the grace of Christ. We are only acceptable to God according to the measure wherein we are like unto his son, Jesus. Christ's divine sonship gives infinite value to his least actions; he is not less adorable nor less pleasing to his Father when he wields the chisel and plane than when he dies upon the cross to save mankind. In us, sanctifying grace, which makes us God's adopted children, deifies all our activity in its root and renders us worthy, like Jesus, although by a different

---

[12] "If I speak in the tongues of men and of angels, but have not love, I am a noisy gong or a clanging cymbal. And if I have prophetic powers, and understand all mysteries and all knowledge, and if I have all faith, so as to remove mountains, but have not love, I am nothing. If I give away all I have, and if I deliver my body to be burned, **but have not love, I gain nothing**" (1 Cor 13:1-3, emphasis added).

title, of his Father's complacency. Sanctifying grace is the first source of our true greatness. It confers upon our life, however commonplace it may seem, its true nobility and imperishable splendor. Oh, if we knew the gift of God!"[13] Without Christ we can do nothing, meaning we cannot do anything spiritually meritorious without him.[14] We can do nothing that benefits us or moves us toward eternal life if it is not done in union with his love and grace living within us. When we enter a state of grace, or receive sanctifying grace, we are changed in quality. We become truly pleasing to God because our sins are removed and we become partakers in his divine life.[15] We become his children by adoption and heirs to the kingdom of heaven. Due to this change in our being, as temples of the Holy Spirit, all of our actions (so long as they are not sinful) become divinized; they are done in grace and therefore have great merit. All of the little, simple activities of our

---

[13] Columba Marmion, *Our Way and Our Life: Christ in His Mysteries*, abridged ed. (Tacoma, WA: Angelico Press, 2013), Kindle edition, loc. 392-398.

[14] "I am the vine, you are the branches. He who abides in me, and I in him, he it is that bears much fruit, for apart from me you can do nothing" (Jn 15:5).

[15] 2 Peter 1:4.

daily life become actions that spread the kingdom of God and his love because of his life within us. The essence of the spirituality of Saint Elizabeth of the Trinity stems from the loving contemplation of sanctifying grace and the life of the Trinity dwelling within us. The essence of the spirituality of Saint Thérèse of Lisieux stemmed from the loving contemplation of the effect that the divine life within us has on even the smallest things that we do. Little things done with great love. The little things are our human actions, the great love is Love himself infusing our actions by his life within us.

Therefore, the first principle, as mentioned in the title of this chapter, is confession and a return to sanctifying grace. It is only in grace that we can have true communion with Jesus in the Eucharist. When we receive holy Communion in grace, Christ finds his own love within us and there is a true intimacy of life. If, God forbid, we receive holy Communion outside of grace and in mortal sin, then the Lord would not find his love in us but rather a love for his enemy, the devil. He would be entering a hostile environment where there is no communion of life and love. Communions like this are an act of handing Jesus over to his enemies, and we eat and drink condemnation upon ourselves.

> *Whoever, therefore, eats the bread or drinks the cup of the Lord in an unworthy manner will be guilty of profaning the body and blood of the Lord. Let a man examine himself, and so eat of the bread and drink of the cup. For anyone who eats and drinks without discerning the body eats and drinks judgment upon himself. That is why many of you are weak and ill, and some have died (1 Cor 11:27-30).*

Sacramental confession is necessary for restoration to grace and to make us worthy of receiving holy Communion. It is the willed choice to leave Jericho and sin behind and unite ourselves to Jesus in the Blessed Sacrament. Leaving Jericho marks the beginning of the spiritual life and entrance into a state of grace. In addition, this principle includes not only the cutting out of mortal sin from our lives, but also a constant striving to cut out all venial sins, faults, and attachments to sin (which will be covered more in the next chapter). We then become disciples of Jesus, children of the heavenly Father, and form part of that multitude that we read is following Christ up to Jerusalem.

THE SECOND PRINCIPLE:
MARIAN CONSECRATION

———————•———————

Bartimaeus, a blind beggar, the son of Timaeus,
was sitting by the roadside . . .
(Mk 10:46).

After leaving Jericho, and thus establishing the principle of confession and a return to grace, we will look at the principle of the necessity for consecration to Our Lady. While it is not immediately evident in this line from the healing of Bartimaeus (the last part of Mark 10:46), I believe its effects are implicitly present: "Bartimaeus, a blind beggar, the son of Timaeus, was sitting by the roadside [side of the way]." This line will form the

29

content of this chapter.

Becoming Children

To begin with, I believe a better translation from the Greek would be "a son of Timaeus, Bartimaeus the blind man, was sitting by the side of the way begging." The Greek word *prosaiteo* is a verb, so "begging" or "to beg" is a better translation than the noun "beggar."

Let's look at the first part, "a son of Timaeus, Bartimaeus the blind man . . ." In Hebrew, the inclusion of the word "bar" before a name means "son of." For instance, "And Jesus answered him [Peter], 'Blessed are you, Simon Bar-Jona! For flesh and blood has not revealed this to you, but my Father who is in heaven'" (Mt 16:17). In this instance, Jesus refers to Simon as the son of Jona. Interestingly, Jesus is also praising the work of the heavenly Father in Peter. Peter is becoming a child of the Father because he is becoming like Christ in the way he acts. Like Jesus, Peter is acting under the inspiration of the heavenly Father. Being comes before act. What something is determines what it does. Our actions reveal whose children we are. Are we children of God, or children of the father of lies? This is seen when

Jesus is speaking with the Pharisees in John 8: "'I speak of what I have seen with my Father, and you do what you have heard from your father.' They answered him, 'Abraham is our father.' Jesus said to them, 'If you were Abraham's children, you would do what Abraham did . . .'" (Jn 8:38-39). Jesus goes on to point out that because they are seeking to kill him, they are therefore children of the devil because they actively seek to accomplish that which the devil desires: ". . . But now you seek to kill me, a man who has told you the truth which I heard from God; this is not what Abraham did. You do what your father did. . . . You are of your father the devil, and your will is to do your father's desires. He was a murderer from the beginning, and has nothing to do with the truth, because there is no truth in him. When he lies, he speaks according to his own nature, for he is a liar and the father of lies" (Jn 8:40-41, 44).

As we said above, when we are baptized we become children of the heavenly Father, and we are filled with his grace and given strength to act according to his will. When we sin, however, we become slaves of the devil and we begin to forget God Our Father. The devil does all he can to make us forget the Father or to think that the

31

Father will never take us back because of what we have done. The memory of our dignity is slowly lost as we slide further down the slope of sin. However, as we read in the Gospel of Luke, when the prodigal son had reached the depths of sin in his own life, it is the memory of his father, and how his father loves, that causes him to seek to restore the relationship. "But when he came to himself he said, 'How many of my father's hired servants have bread enough and to spare, but I perish here with hunger! I will arise and go to my father . . .'" (Lk 15:17-18). He had thought that after all he had done, and because he had been living as a slave to sin for so long, he would only be able to return to his father's house as a slave. However, when he arrives home, it is mercy that awaits him and the father receives him back not as a slave but as his son.

Our battle with the demonic is primarily a battle of ideas or principles. Higher demonic activity is focused on trying to get us to accept false ideas about ourselves or God as true. Once these false ideas or principles are believed as true, they lead to conclusions and consequences that are disastrous. Ideas have consequences. The devil wants us to forget whose we are, to whom we belong, and how highly we are valued by God. God loves and values us so much that he is willing to purchase us back through the death of his Son. "For God so loved the world that he gave his only Son" (Jn 3:16). If we want to know how much God values us we have only to look at the cross. The devil wants us to think of ourselves not as what we are, but as what we lack or according to the worst sins we have committed. This is summed up in "a son of Timaeus, Bartimaeus the blind man . . ." *Bar* means "son of." So "a son of Timaeus" and "Bartimaeus" mean the same thing; it's like a repetition or emphasis on the relationship to his father. If we investigate the meaning of the name *Timaeus*, we find this battle over who we are and who we belong to within the name itself. There are some who say that the name originates from the Hebrew word *Tamé*, meaning "impure" or "unclean"; others say it is derived from the Greek word *Timaios*, meaning "highly prized" or "greatly valued." So, in a certain sense, it can represent a battle over whose he will be in the end. This highlights the important truth that whom we will belong to in the end is not yet fixed. Even though we may have left sin behind, it would be foolishly presumptuous to think ourselves no longer capable of sin. To believe we are safe from sin is evidence of very poor self-knowledge. Our capacity for sanctity is matched by a capacity for much evil. We are not in a state of "once saved, always saved"; rather, we "work out our salvation with fear and trembling."[16] There can also be no standing still in the spiritual life—if we are not moving forward we are becoming worse. That is why the temptation comes to sit down, because the devil knows that if he can get us to stop moving forward because of fear or laziness, then we will begin to slide backward. The name Timaeus also represents the battle in terms of how we see ourselves. Do we see the true dignity of our *being* as children of God, or are we always plagued by past sinful actions, even when confessed, and see ourselves only as the worst things we have ever done? Are we "highly valued" or "impure and unclean"?

The case for the translation of "highly prized" or "greatly valued" seems to be the stronger of the two. That which is most "highly prized" should be God. He is the pearl beyond all price, and when we find him we should

---

[16] "Therefore, my beloved, as you have always obeyed, so now, not only as in my presence but much more in my absence, work out your own salvation with fear and trembling" (Phil 2:12).

sell all we have to "purchase" him and his kingdom. We purchase the kingdom of God through the merits of the death of his Son. Bartimaeus sees himself according to his lack of sight as "the blind man," but our dignity derives principally from our being. Our ability to act and what we are capable of is based on our nature. A fallen human nature is not capable of meritorious and great acts, but someone in a state of grace can move mountains. In a state of grace our nature is mingled with the divine and what is normally impossible for us "is possible with God" (Lk 18:27). In grace we can truly say, "I can do all things in him who strengthens me" (Phil 4:13). All hell trembles before a humble, confident, and trusting soul that is in a state of grace because of what that soul is now capable of due to the Trinity dwelling within it.

Bartimaeus, in a sense, measures what he is capable of only by what he lacks and not by God's grace, which can do all things. He is blind exteriorly but also lacks interior light. In the spiritual sense, he is in grace, but he does not yet truly know himself or his own dignity as a child of the Father, nor does he know the Father. This is why, in the spiritual life, what follows purgation or the purgative way is illumination or the illuminative way. This is both active and passive on the part of the soul. The inflow of light—which is Christ as truth—into the intellect through the illuminative way reveals to us who we truly are and who God truly is. When we stand in the light of truth himself, we receive humbling self-knowledge of our misery, mixed with awe-inspiring knowledge of his mercy and majesty! This was the secure foundation given to Saint Catherine of Siena by the Lord when he revealed to her the truth that would save her from all error and keep her safe from evil. "Do you know, daughter, who you are, and who I am? If you know these two things, you will be blessed. You are she who is not; whereas I am he who is. Have this knowledge in your soul and the enemy will never deceive you and you will escape all his wiles; you will never disobey my commandments and will acquire all grace, truth, and light."[17]

Becoming Perfect

Once sins are absolved in confession they are truly

---

[17] Raymond of Capua, *The Life of St. Catherine of Siena: the Classic on Her Life and Accomplishments as Recorded by Her Spiritual Director* (Charlotte, North Carolina: TAN Books, 2011), Kindle edition, 62.

washed away in the Blood of Christ. There remain, however, the wounds from sin that need to be healed and attachments that need to be uprooted. We are forgiven, but not yet made perfect. Serious sins carry serious wounds, and the process of healing them can take a long time. The devil tries to keep us in serious sin in order for that sin to wound us more and more deeply. His desire is that our sin will remain unconfessed, therefore unforgiven, and that we will die in that state. Before sin, the devil tempts with presumption on God's mercy. After the sin is committed, he tempts with despair of ever being forgiven by God. Before sin, the temptation is to reduce the significance of serious sin to something insignificant. After sin, the temptation is to exaggerate the sin to something that is beyond the power of the infinite mercy of God to forgive. When a soul does confess sin, the devil then moves on to tempt it with a fear of not having the means to attain the goal of perfection. He points out our weakness, he accuses us of all the sinful things we have done and the good things we have failed to do. He tells us it is pride to think we could ever become really holy, when it is really a subtle form of pride and self-reliance to think that we can't. And so, like Bartimaeus, we can choose to sit down beside the way and become content with being good instead of becoming perfect. We can be set free from mortal sin but then do no more. We can choose to receive all the love and forgiveness of God but show no love in return. "In order to be good, a man must be filled with love, and to be devout, he must further be very ready and apt to perform the deeds of love."[18] We can be filled with God's love, which makes us good, but never become devout—as his love demands—and therefore never become perfect. It should be obvious that by choosing this "sitting down" or stagnation, we open ourselves to many serious dangers and consequences.

Firstly, the danger with this choice to sit down and settle is that we remain dangerously close to Jericho—far too close for comfort. By not mortifying our desires and attachments, by not growing in virtue, the temptation to return to sin will overpower us. If we do not amend our lives, mortify our desires, and sever our attachments, or if we make no effort to eliminate occasions of sin, then it

---

[18] Francis of Sales, *Introduction to the Devout Life - Enhanced Version* (Christian Classics Ethereal Library, 2009), Kindle edition, loc. 217-218.

should not be surprising for us to fall backward into old habits. Samson did not flee the occasion of sin, and therefore all his supernatural strength was taken from him while he slept. "And he [Samson] awoke from his sleep, and said, 'I will go out as at other times, and shake myself free.' And he did not know that the Lord had left him" (Jgs 16:20). In the same way, if we linger in occasions of sin, we will be lulled into a false security and our supernatural strength (sanctifying grace) will be snatched from us while we are asleep and not keeping watch. We will then be bound and taken prisoner to sin.

Secondly, the other serious danger is that we will become indifferent to what is holy and sacred. We will become indifferent to Jesus present in the Eucharist in the same way that the Israelites began to loath the manna because of the desire for the food of Egypt that was still in their hearts. Their longing for earthly food made them complain about the heavenly food. If our lives are not purified from living only to satisfy our senses, then we will not love Jesus as we should in the Eucharist, where his real presence is not experienced by the senses but known by faith. Mass and eucharistic adoration will be in danger of becoming a chore instead of an intimate encounter of communion with the living God. The Mass will become only one other thing in our weekly schedule instead of the pinnacle of every day.

We are not called to be simply smoldering embers but blazing fires of love![19] The most tragic consequence of remaining sitting beside the way is that we will become neither hot nor cold, neither hating what is evil nor loving what is good, but rather indifferently lukewarm. In the Book of Revelation, the Lord says to the members of the Church in Laodicea, "I know your works: you are neither cold nor hot. Would that you were cold or hot! So, because you are lukewarm, and neither cold nor hot, I will spew you out of my mouth" (Rv 3:15-16). The Lord describes them as being "wretched, pitiable, poor, blind, and naked" (Rv 3:17), a description that could be similarly applied to Bartimaeus in his current state. The solution given to them by the Lord is the universal remedy to all

---

[19] "The difference between love and devotion is just that which exists between fire and flame;—love being a spiritual fire which becomes devotion when it is fanned into a flame;—and what devotion adds to the fire of love is that flame which makes it eager, energetic, and diligent, not merely in obeying God's commandments, but in fulfilling his divine counsels and inspirations" Francis of Sales, *Introduction to the Devout Life*, loc. 223-226.

those settled in lukewarmness. "Therefore I counsel you to buy from me gold refined by fire, that you may be rich; and white garments to clothe you and to keep the shame of your nakedness from being seen; and salve to anoint your eyes, that you may see" (Rv 3:18). The gold refined by fire is his sacred flesh that passed through the fire of his Passion. This is Jesus in the Blessed Sacrament, and we "purchase" this fire-tried gold through our participation in the offering of his holy sacrifice. The white garments represent a soul in sanctifying grace, because in grace our shame or nakedness is washed away by the Blood of Christ. We "buy" this garment through the reception of Baptism or absolution in sacramental confession. The salve used to anoint our eyes, in order that we may see, is holy scripture. Faith comes through the hearing of the word. The eyes of faith are opened through the hearing of scripture and we begin to truly see. These three things represent our full, active, and worthy participation in the holy sacrifice of the Mass. We have to approach the mystery with a white garment, meaning in a state of grace. Then we receive the salve that anoints our eyes in the Liturgy of the Word and the gold refined by fire in the Liturgy of the Eucharist.

There is effort required in sanctification; but our efforts made in cooperation with God's grace will bring us healing. For our part, we must open wide the doors to Christ, the doors of our hearts. This means that, like opening a door, we remove everything that stands between us and Jesus and full transforming union with him. We remove all the lesser loves that block us from loving him completely. When we do this, he will come to us and live in intimacy with us. "Behold, I stand at the door and knock; if anyone hears my voice and opens the door, I will come in to him and eat with him, and he with me" (Rv 3:20). When we start to return love for love, mortifying ourselves and growing in virtue and holiness, we walk further away from the allure of Jericho and closer toward Jesus where he is present in the Eucharist. There has not been a saint in the Church who was not centered on the Blessed Sacrament. Through mortification of the senses, our eyes of faith are opened and we begin to see that the greatest good, the only thing worth living and dying for, is Jesus in the Blessed Sacrament. The Eucharist is the source of all strength and grace for our spiritual lives; if we do not live from this heavenly food we will not grow in sanctity. Saint Catherine hungered so deeply for holy Communion that, when she saw her spiritual director and confessor, she would cry out, "Father, I'm hungry! For the love of God, give my soul its food!"[20]

A Mother's Care

There are two types of life we receive. Both come to us through a father and a mother, and both require nourishment in order to grow and flourish. These two lives are our natural life and our supernatural life. Our natural life begins at conception. We receive this life from our parents and it requires food and nourishment in order to grow. When this natural life begins we are completely dependent on our parents for everything. Our spiritual life, however, begins at Baptism, when we receive the life of God into us. This life comes to us from the Father and our mother the Church. The nourishment or food of the supernatural life is the Eucharist. Like the beginnings of our natural life, our spiritual life is fragile when it begins and requires a mother's special care and protection. We

[20] Raymond of Capua, *The Life of St. Catherine of Siena: the Classic on Her Life and Accomplishments as Recorded by Her Spiritual Director* (Charlotte, North Carolina: TAN Books, 2011), Kindle edition, 257.

are always in need of holy mother Church, through which we receive Christ and his sacraments; but we also need the particular and special care of Mary, mother of God and mother of the Church. We are helpless spiritual infants in need of being carried. In a spiritual sense this is where we find Bartimaeus. He is outside of Jericho, but he is sitting beside the way begging. Instead of walking on the way he is immobile beside it and helpless. He has begun the journey but lacks the courage to go on up to Jerusalem. He is in need of his Mother.

The journey to perfection is long and difficult. "The ordinary purification, whether of body or soul, is only accomplished by slow degrees, step by step, gradually and painfully."[21] When we see the way stretched out before us with all its dangers, mixed with a knowledge of our own weakness, we are tempted to despair of ever reaching where the great saints have found rest. The Lord Jesus knows our weaknesses and fears that cause us to lose hope of progress in holiness; and so he left us with the two great gifts given during his passion and death: the gift of himself in the Eucharist, given on the night that began

---

[21] Francis of Sales, *Introduction to the Devout Life - Enhanced Version*, Kindle edition, loc. 348-349.

his passion; and the gift of his Mother, given in the final moments of his agony. Saint Teresa of Avila speaks beautifully of the gift of Jesus himself in the Eucharist, which gives us courage to persevere in faith and grow in holiness. She says that "the good Jesus knew what he had given for us and how important it was for us to give this to God, and yet how difficult it would be for us to do so, as has been said, because of our natural inclination to base things and our want of love and courage. He saw that, before we could be aroused, we needed his aid, not once but every day, and it must have been for this reason that he resolved to remain with us."[22] She says also, in speaking of Jesus in the Blessed Sacrament, ". . . if we profit by his company, we shall also have him in heaven, for the only reason he remains with us is to help and encourage and sustain us so that we shall do that will, which, as we have said, is to be fulfilled in us."[23] To better appreciate the gift of Christ himself in the Eucharist, to adore him more worthily and to contemplate his eucharistic face more truly, we have to adore and

[22] Saint Teresa of Avila, *The Way of Perfection by Saint Teresa of Avila* (Ignacio Hills Press, 2009), Kindle edition, 101.

[23] Ibid., 104.

contemplate him with Mary. This was the mission given by Saint John Paul II to the whole Church. "To contemplate the face of Christ, and to contemplate it with Mary, is the 'programme' which I have set before the Church at the dawn of the third millennium, summoning her to put out into the deep on the sea of history with the enthusiasm of the new evangelization. To contemplate Christ involves being able to recognize him wherever he manifests himself, in his many forms of presence, but above all in the living sacrament of his body and his blood. *The Church draws her life from Christ in the Eucharist*, by him she is fed and by him she is enlightened."[24] This contemplation of Jesus in the Eucharist with Mary is the fountain from which the new evangelization springs. Therefore we must consecrate ourselves to Mary in order to more perfectly adore her Son. We must mingle our prayers with hers, and place our hearts in the blazing furnace of the immaculate heart so that they may catch fire. The gift of Mary helps us to better appreciate the gift of the Eucharist. Mary fills us with courage and zeal for Christ and all that belongs to him. She fills us with a deep

---

[24] *Ecclesia De Eucharistia,* § 6.

desire to become holy and pleasing to God.

Bartimaeus and Dante

We can see the effects of courage and zeal that the Marian influence has on our lives by looking at some fascinating parallels between Bartimaeus and where we find Dante at the beginning of the *Inferno* in Cantos 1 and 2. The account of the healing of Bartimaeus gives the exterior details of what happened; whereas the first two Cantos can serve as an analogy for the interior and spiritual activities. Like any analogy it is not perfect—but that is the nature of analogy. Both are stories of souls drawing closer to Christ, and this path has certain principles that are always true. These principles can be seen in both Bartimaeus and Dante. We find Dante has lost hope of attaining the mountain of paradise and perfection, and so he turns back in despair. A look into what gives him the courage to set out on the journey will help us see the importance of Marian consecration as the second principle of the spiritual life.

In Canto 1, Dante has left the life of sin behind, but he finds himself in a dark forest because he wandered from the way, like Bartimaeus, who has left Jericho but is in blind darkness and is sitting beside the way. Dante moves to ascend the mountain but the three beasts, representing the threefold concupiscence, cause him to lose hope of climbing the mountain, and he gives up in fear. The leopard represents lust, the lion pride, and the wolf avarice. These are what Saint John refers to when he says, "For all that is in the world, the lust of the flesh and the lust of the eyes and the pride of life, is not of the Father but is of the world" (1 Jn 2:16). They are disordered desires within us as a consequence of original sin that must be brought under control. This threefold concupiscence of the wolf, leopard, and lion needs to be tamed by Christ and made subject to him. This is what Isaiah speaks of when he says, "The wolf shall dwell with the lamb, and the leopard shall lie down with the kid, and the calf and the lion and the fatling together, and a little child shall lead them" (Is 11:6).

There are also all of the other evil desires and attachments, which stem from the three principle ones, that cry out in us until they are mortified and put to silence. They are desires that cry out to be satisfied but are being denied and left in darkness, like Bartimaeus who is begging or crying out, but is left unfulfilled in these lower desires. These desires have to be put to sleep in Bartimaeus so that he can move from begging for many things to begging for the one thing necessary, the mercy of God. Sitting in his darkness and hopelessness, Bartimaeus encounters light himself and cries out for mercy. Dante's own words describe his encounter with Virgil with mysterious similitude. He says:

> *Now while I stumbled to the deepest wood,*
> *before my eyes appeared the form of one*
> *who seemed hoarse, having held his words so long.*
> *And when I saw him in that endless waste,*
> *"Mercy upon me, mercy!" I cried out . . .*[25]

Dante asks to be lead to Saint Peter's gate and the canto ends with, "He set on, and I held my pace behind." This is like Bartimaeus who, after being healed by Christ "followed him on the way" to the gate of Jerusalem. Dante will walk behind Virgil like Bartimaeus will end up following Christ on the way. However, almost as soon as the journey is begun, doubt creeps into Dante's heart, and he asks if he has the spiritual strength to make this

---

[25] Dante Alighieri, *The Inferno*, ed. and trans. Anthony M. Esolen and Gustave Doré, The Modern Library Classics (New York: Modern Library, 2005), 7.

journey. After Dante questions his ability to reach the goal, seeing himself to be insignificant and miserable, he receives firm courage to press on based on what Virgil tells him. Virgil says to him:

> *"If I have understood your words aright,"*
> *replied the shade of that greathearted man,*
> *"your spirit has been bruised by cowardice,*
> *which many a time so weighs a man's heart down*
> *it turns him from a glorious enterprise—*
> *as shadows fool the horse that shies away.*
> *That you may slip this worry and go free,*
> *I'll tell you why I came and what I heard*
> *when first I pitied you your misery."*[26]

Virgil goes on to say that the reason he is there to help Dante is because Mary has had pity on him. "A gentle Lady in heaven was so moved with pity for that soul whose way is barred, she broke the rigid sentence from above."[27] When Dante realizes that he is loved by Mary he is set on fire with courage. Mary sends Saint Lucy to help Dante, who is himself described as a faithful

---

[26] Ibid., 15.

[27] Ibid., 19.

follower of Lucy. Saint Lucy is the patron saint of those who are blind—yet another detail linking Dante with the blind Bartimaeus. Dante's response at the end of Canto 2 is again remarkably similar to what we see in actions of Bartimaeus after his healing. Dante says:

> *I cried out as a man at last set free,*
> *"O lady of compassion and my help!*
> *And you most gracious who obeyed her wish*
> *soon as you heard the truth she spoke to you!*
> *Your words have put my heart in order now,*
> *kindling so great a longing to set on*
> *you've turned me to our first intention—go!*
> *Go, for we two now share one will alone:*
> *you are my guide, my teacher, and my lord."*[28]

Mary, Model of the Interior Life

King David continually asked the Lord "to strengthen his heart against cowardice and discouragement; and it is our privilege in this war that we are certain to vanquish so long as we are willing to fight."[29] Knowing that Mary

---

[28] Ibid., 21.

[29] Francis of Sales, *Introduction to the Devout Life - Enhanced Version*, Kindle edition, loc. 365-366.

loves us—and experiencing the comfort that comes through consecration to her—sets our hearts on fire with courage for the fight. We receive an increased trust in God's providence to provide sufficient grace at every moment. Mary puts our hearts in order because her immaculate heart is perfectly ordered. "Our Lord loved her [Mary's] heart more than all other hearts put together, and was in turn loved by it more perfectly than by the hearts of all the Seraphim. What union, what intimacy, what understanding, what correspondence between these two hearts! What fire in these two furnaces of love constantly inflamed by the breath of the Holy Spirit!"[30] Mary's heart and Mary's love were always perfectly directed toward her Son because he is her heart and her love. Therefore, she fixes our hearts on Jesus in the same way. Mary models our interior life based on hers. "There is an old sixth-century Byzantine painting of the most Blessed Virgin that gives a perfect subject of meditation; the heart of Mary as the consummate ideal of the apostolate. The figure of Our Blessed Lady is shown carrying in her bosom the Incarnate Word surrounded by

---

[30] Jean Eudes, *The Admirable Heart of Mary*, trans. Ruth Hauser (Fort Erie, Ont.: Immaculate Heart of Mary, 2007), 15.

a circle of light. Like the eternal Father she ever keeps within herself the Word she has given to the world. As Rohault de Fleury said: 'The Savior shines in the midst of her breast like the Eucharist with all the veils torn away.' Jesus lives in her. He is her heart, her life-breath, her center, and her life: this is an image of the interior life."[31]

Love itself is so powerful that we grow in equality and likeness to the things we love. We become what we love! This is wonderful if we love God above all things; but tragic if we love anything less than him, more than him. Scripture says of the Israelites that "they came to Ba'al-pe'or, and consecrated themselves to Ba'al, and became detestable like the thing they loved" (Hos 9:10). Saint John of the Cross says of those who "are attached to the things of the world. He [God] calls them little ones because they become as little as the things they love."[32] He says further: "a person is indeed ignorant if he thinks it is possible to reach this high state of union with God

[31] Dom Jean-Baptiste Chautard, *Soul of the Apostolate* (TAN Books, 1977), Kindle edition, 295.

[32] Saint John of the Cross, *The Collected Works of St. John of the Cross*, 2d ed., ICS Publications (Washington, D. C.: Institute of Carmelite Studies, 1979), 81.

without first emptying his appetite of all the natural and supernatural things which can be a hindrance to him. For there is an extreme distance between such appetites and that which is given in this state, which is nothing less than transformation in God."[33] So Mary helps us to stop begging for the lesser loves and fix in our hearts pure love of God alone. Pure love of God above all things, and love of all things for his sake, makes us like God. Our Lady turns us back to our first intention, the intention to become holy, which we give up because of fear. This fear is based on self-reliance and a lack of trust in God to finish the work of holiness that he has begun in us through Baptism. This self-reliance takes its root in pride, and in pride we spend our time looking for the answer within ourselves. We see the enormity of the task of becoming saints and give up because it is beyond our strength. We choose to settle with a good life instead of a saintly life because the means to get there seem to be out of our reach; but Mary shows us that the necessary strength is only as far away as the nearest tabernacle or monstrance. Regarding holiness and sanctity: the

---

[33] Ibid., 81.

beginning, the end, and the means to get there is Jesus in the Eucharist. He is the source, the summit, and the way. To be a disciple of Christ we must renounce everything we have for the sake of the Eucharist, which is Christ, because without him we have nothing. The Lord makes this clear when he says:

> *Whoever does not bear his own cross and come after me, cannot be my disciple. For which of you, desiring to build a tower, does not first sit down and count the cost, whether he has enough to complete it? Otherwise, when he has laid a foundation, and is not able to finish, all who see it begin to mock him, saying, 'This man began to build, and was not able to finish.' Or what king, going to encounter another king in war, will not sit down first and take counsel whether he is able with ten thousand to meet him who comes against him with twenty thousand? And if not, while the other is yet a great way off, he sends an embassy and asks terms of peace. So therefore, whoever of you does not renounce all that he has cannot be my disciple (Lk 14:27-33).*

If we build alone, we build in vain, and anything we attempt will fail. If we go to war alone against the great evil that is without and within we will be conquered.

"Unless the Lord builds the house, those who build it labor in vain. Unless the Lord watches over the city, the watchman stays awake in vain" (Ps 127:1). Mystically, the building of a tower is the ascent in the spiritual life, building upward and closer toward perfect union with God. Mary shows us by her own example in scripture how to build a tower that reaches heaven. She simply gave her *fiat* for the Word to accomplish everything in her. "Be it done unto me according to thy word" (Lk 1:38). And with her consent, the Word became flesh within her, and the tower that unites heaven and earth was built. The Eucharist is that same flesh, that same tower. The humility of Mary counters our pride. She teaches us to allow the Word to sanctify us, most especially when the Word made flesh is within us in holy Communion or when we are kneeling before him in eucharistic adoration. The "king, going to encounter another king in war" also mystically represents the spiritual battle for growth in holiness. Again, it is the humble example of Mary that shows us that we don't win this battle by remaining as kings or rulers of our own lives, but rather by renouncing everything and becoming servants of the Lord. If we make him king and submit ourselves to his eucharistic reign, which is the reign of our humble king, then all pride will be conquered and he will win the war in us. When we stand fearful before what appears to be an overwhelming army, Mary seems to speak to our hearts, not through audible words but through the conviction that her presence brings, saying, "do not worry, child; the God of power and majesty is with you in the Eucharist. And if he is for you, who can stand against you?"

Mary the Maidservant

An infallible fruit of true Marian devotion is an increased love of the holy sacrifice of the Mass and the Blessed Sacrament. The Mass is the sacrifice that obtains every remedy for our lukewarm souls, and it is Mary who leads us into the depths of the sacrifice of her Son. In chapter 18 of John's Gospel he mentions a "maidservant" who keeps the gate of the high priest's house. John, who entered with Jesus, goes and speaks to the maidservant of the high priest so that Peter, who is standing outside, will be allowed to enter into the place where Jesus is undergoing his passion. Mary refers to herself similarly in her Magnificat when she says that the Lord has "regarded the low estate of his maidservant" (Lk 1:48). In a very real sense Mary is the maidservant who keeps the gate to the high priest's house. It is through her that we gain access to the depths of Christ's passion. It was only those who were united with her who were able to persevere all the way up Calvary to the foot of the cross. She leads us to the Mass, and we stand at the foot of the cross with her, and she says to our hearts, "Look how much he loves you!" Her heart *is* the house of Christ the high priest because he dwells within it, and therein are contained all of his mysteries. Mary controls the gate to her heart and who may enter into it. Mary is not only the gatekeeper to Christ's passion but also to all the mysteries of his life, which she held continually pondering them in her heart. "Unerring experience has told us that we never advance more rapidly in love of the Son than when we travel by the Mother, and that what we have built most solidly in Jesus has been built with Mary. There is no time lost in seeking him, if we go at once to Mary, for he is always there, always at home. The darkness in his mysteries becomes light when we hold it to her light, which is his light as well. She is the short road to him. She has the 'grand entry' to him. She is his Esther, and speedy and full are the answers to the petitions her hand presents."[34] If we want to find the Lord we should go to Mary, because the words the Angel Gabriel spoke at the Annunciation are always true: "Hail, full of grace, the Lord is with you!" (Lk 1:28). The Lord is always with her. The first activity of Mary, once Jesus was conceived, was to bring his veiled presence (veiled within her) to those whom she knew to be in need (Elizabeth, Zachariah, and the unborn John). When she greets them, the Holy Spirit causes Saint John and Saint Elizabeth to recognize the veiled Christ. In a similar way, the first thing Mary does when we bring her into our lives, working in complete union with the Holy Spirit, is to cause us to recognize the veiled Christ, not hidden within her womb but behind the eucharistic veil. Mary's only desire is to place her Son at the center of our lives. Her longing is that the Eucharist, which is Jesus, becomes our beginning and end, the source and summit of our life and love.

Bartimaeus doesn't see Jesus because he's blind. In fact, he doesn't sense Jesus's presence in any way. Rather he hears that it is Jesus, and he believes what he has

---

[34] Father Frederick Faber, *The Foot of the Cross with Mary: or The Sorrows of Mary* (KIC, 2015), Kindle Edition, loc. 149-153.

heard. In the same way, we don't see Jesus in the Blessed Sacrament nor sense him with any of the other senses. We hear, and thus know by faith, that he is there. Without seeing, Bartimaeus believes; and his belief and faith lead him to receive sight. We are called to do the same, "for we walk by faith, not by sight" (2 Cor 5:7). This living faith in us will flower into the vision of God. Even though we don't see him now, faith becomes vision for those who have persevered in grace and love to the end. And so it is both faith and works of faith that are required for final vision; just as Bartimaeus had to stand up and walk to Jesus while still blind in order to receive healing. The courage to act in faith comes to us through the woman of faith. Jesus did not have faith; he always had the vision of the Father. At the foot of the cross, Mary "sees the hand of God where even the most believing see only darkness and desolation. Hers was the greatest act of faith ever elicited by a creature, a faith higher than that of the angels when they were as yet in their period of trial."[35] As Father Faber describes so beautifully: "How greatly

---

[35] Rev. Reginald Garrigou-Lagrange, OP, *The Mother of the Saviour: and Our Interior Life* (Catholic Way Publishing, 2013), Kindle edition, 221.

then must she have rejoiced in the magnificent supernatural acts which her sorrows were causing her to elicit all the while! Such faith, such hope, such love, such fortitude, such conformity, such love of suffering, such spirit of sacrifice, such intelligent worship, such incomparable union! Millions of saints could have been made out of each of these royal magnificences, and yet have left a marvelous amount to spare."[36]

For souls stuck in despair or who have become arrogantly presumptuous, Mary brings the theological virtue of hope. Hope raises us up from dark despair or lowers us down from prideful presumption. For souls lost in doubt or darkness of mind, Mary brings the virtue of faith. When souls have become stagnant, fearful, and self-seeking, Mary brings love in order to embolden the soul for sacrifice, which is the proof of love. What we see in Bartimaeus seems to be the fruit of a "Marian intervention" either by her or someone acting on her behalf. "When Mary is living in the heart of her apostle, he will be guaranteed the use of the persuasive eloquence of Our Blessed Mother herself, speaking in him, and

[36] Father Frederick Faber, *The Foot of the Cross with Mary: or The Sorrows of Mary*, Kindle Edition, loc. 973.

moving souls with whom all else has failed. It is apparent that Our Lord, in a most beautiful delicacy of feeling, has left to the mediation of his Mother the most difficult conquests of the apostolate desiring that they should be accorded to no one but those who live in intimate union with her."[37] Maybe it was Mary who told Bartimaeus that her Son was close by. It is highly possible that she would have been in this group heading with Jesus from Galilee to Jerusalem for Passover. In the same way, when we have given up and are losing hope, Mary whispers to us, "Jesus of Nazareth is passing by. He is the fulfillment of all your desires; go after him with all your heart because he is worth it all!" To look into Mary's face causes love to catch fire and faith to become bold. She gives us a renewed reverence and love for the Mass because no one else, besides Jesus, knows or felt the weight of the Crucifixion like she did. No one appreciates the price of our salvation or values Christ's sacrificial offering more than Mary does. She felt the death of her Son more acutely than all the saints combined, precisely because she is his mother. "She lives in Jesus, through Jesus, by his

---

[37] Chautard, *Soul of the Apostolate*, Kindle edition, 291.

life, his love, and by union with his sacrifice; and Jesus speaks in her and through her. Jesus is her life, and she is the Word-carrier, she amplifies his voice, she serves as his monstrance."[38]

To Jesus Through Mary

Mary is not an optional but a necessary element of our spiritual lives. The Lord came into the world through Mary; he wills to come to us through her. It is the work of the Holy Spirit and Mary that causes Christ to grow within us. "Two sanctifiers are necessary to souls, the Holy Spirit and the Virgin Mary, for they are the only ones who can reproduce Christ . . . The first is the Sanctifier by essence . . . Mary, for her part, is the cooperator, the indispensable instrument in and by God's design . . . These two, then, the Holy Spirit and Mary, are the indispensable artificers of Jesus, the indispensable sanctifiers of souls."[39] We receive the Holy Spirit through Baptism and absolution. It is important that we also turn our hearts to Mary through a willed consecration. "We

[38] Ibid., 296.

[39] Luis M. Martínez, *The Sanctifier*, [2nd ed. (Boston, MA: Pauline Books & Media, 2003), 6-7.

must know her in order to know him [Jesus]. As there is no true devotion to his sacred humanity, which is not mindful of his divinity, so there is no adequate love of the Son, which disjoins him from his Mother and lays her aside as a mere instrument, whom God chose as he might choose an inanimate thing, without regard to its sanctity or moral fitness."[40] We are never truly pleasing eucharistic adorers until we adore with Mary. When we adore Jesus with Mary, our prayer becomes irresistible to his heart because we pray with her. The purpose of Marian consecration is to make the eucharistic Christ the center of our lives and to reach a deeper intimacy with him than is possible without her.

After the fall, God said that he would put enmity between Satan and the woman. At Cana and at the foot of the cross is where Jesus calls Mary "woman." Where there is enmity there is no middle ground. There is no gray area, there is no place to stand and say, "I'm not for the devil, but I'm not comfortable with Mary." Any uncomfortable feelings or any apprehension toward giving oneself completely to Mary do not come from

---

[40] Father Frederick Faber, *The Foot of the Cross with Mary: or The Sorrows of Mary*, Kindle Edition, loc. 138-141.

God. He leads us by his own example in entrusting ourselves completely to Mary. He dwelt within her; he was nourished, clothed, and protected by her. Jesus's life on earth began with Mary and ended with Mary. We should live every day in that same way. We should become more like Jesus and begin all things with Mary and finish them with her too. This is therefore the second principle: namely, a consecration to Mary, preferably through either the formula of Saint Louis Marie de Montfort or Saint Maximilian Kolbe. Both formulas offer proper preparation of mind and heart to make the consecration of oneself to Mary. Following this we should renew a simple prayer of consecration daily to Mary, placing ourselves on the right side of the eternal enmity. The daily consecration reminds us of what we have promised, and it helps us to interiorize the consecration so that it is not only exterior words but also a complete wholehearted gift of ourselves. Daily consecration gives Mary permission to draw us closer to the Eucharist.

Totus Tuus

Immaculate Conception, Mary my Mother,

Live in me,

Act in me,

Speak in me and through me,

Think your thoughts in my mind,

Love through my heart,

Give me your dispositions and feelings,

Teach, lead me and guide me to Jesus,

Correct, enlighten, and expand my thoughts and behavior,

Possess my soul,

Take over my entire personality and life, replace it with yourself,

Incline me to constant adoration,

Pray in me and through me,

Let me live in you and keep me in this union always. Amen.[41]

---

[41] Jason Evert, *Saint John Paul the Great: His Five Loves* (Lakewood, CO: Totus Tuus Press, 2014), Kindle edition, loc. 2185-2197.

THE THIRD PRINCIPLE:
EUCHARISTIC ADORATION

———————— • ————————

And when he heard that it was Jesus of Nazareth, he began to cry
out and say, "Jesus, Son of David, have mercy on me!" And many
rebuked him, telling him to be silent; but he cried out all the more,
"Son of David, have mercy on me!" And Jesus stopped and said,
"Call him" (Mk 10:47-49).

We come to know that Christ is present in the
Eucharist in the same way that Bartimaeus hears that
Jesus is there. The truth of the real presence of Jesus in
the Blessed Sacrament is something we come to know by
faith, and faith comes through hearing. We know that he
is there, because we have heard it through the words of
Christ himself in scripture and through the teachings of

the bride of Christ, the Church. We believe Christ to be who he says he is—namely, the Son of God. We believe also that he not only speaks truth, but that he is truth. So when he says that "my flesh is real food, and my blood is real drink," and, further, "unless you eat the flesh of the Son of man and drink his blood, you have no life in you," we know that this is not only true but also that Jesus possesses the power to work this miracle because he is God.[42]

In Saint John's gospel, we read of two miracles—or "signs" as John refers to them—the Lord works around the feast of Passover on two consecutive years. Firstly, Jesus works the miracle of the wedding feast of Cana, which was also the first of his signs and marks the

---

[42] "'I am the living bread which came down from heaven; if anyone eats of this bread, he will live forever; and the bread which I shall give for the life of the world is my flesh.' The Jews then disputed among themselves, saying, 'How can this man give us his flesh to eat?' So Jesus said to them, 'Truly, truly, I say to you, unless you eat the flesh of the Son of man and drink his blood, you have no life in you; he who eats my flesh and drinks my blood has eternal life, and I will raise him up at the last day. For my flesh is food indeed, and my blood is drink indeed. He who eats my flesh and drinks my blood abides in me, and I in him. As the living Father sent me, and I live because of the Father, so he who eats me will live because of me. This is the bread which came down from heaven, not such as the fathers ate and died; he who eats this bread will live forever'" (Jn 6:51-58).

beginning of his public life. The following year, again close to the feast of Passover (which John is careful to mention both times), is the miracle of the feeding of the five thousand. When John calls them signs, he does not mean they are not miracles; rather, while they are true miracles, they are also signs, not only of who Christ is, but also of a later and far more beautiful miracle that Christ will work on the Passover of the third year. The miracle of Cana and the feeding of the five thousand are signs prefiguring the institution of the most holy Eucharist.

At Cana, the Lord shows his power over matter. He is able to substantially change one thing into another, water into wine. He is the word through whom all things were created. He has power over all that is, because he created all that is. And so we believe that the One who changed water to wine can just as easily change wine to blood. At Cana, the Lord also manifests his power over time. He is both God and man, both divine and human. In him time meets eternity. While he is in time due to his human nature, he is also outside of time due to his divine nature. And so, even though his hour had not yet come, he has the power to mysteriously link the pending hour of his Passion to the miracle of the wedding feast. "This hour is not yet come; that was the first thing that had to be said. And yet Jesus has the power to anticipate this 'hour' in a mysterious sign. This stamps the miracle of Cana as an anticipation of the hour, tying the two together intrinsically."[43] It is by this same power over time that he is then able to link his once-offered sacrifice on Calvary to every Mass celebrated by the Church. It is not a different sacrifice that is offered in each Mass but the same sacrifice.

The miracle of the feeding of the five thousand teaches us two further important truths about the Eucharist. Firstly, the Lord feeds the people through the hands of his apostles, prefiguring how he will feed the Church through the hands of his priests. Secondly, everyone eats until they are satisfied and yet the bread has not diminished, prefiguring how with every host and in every holy Communion we receive the Lord wholly and entirely, body, blood, soul, and divinity; and yet the Lord is in no way diminished or slowly consumed. The

---

[43] Pope Benedict XVI, *Jesus of Nazareth: from the Baptism in the Jordan to the Transfiguration* (New York: Doubleday, 2007), Kindle edition, 251.

consecrated host can be fractured down to the smallest visible particles and in each particle the Lord is truly, completely, really, and substantially present.

Beyond Obligation

Our eucharistic faith is based on our belief that Christ is God and that he speaks the truth. We believe that the Lord Jesus is present in the Blessed Sacrament because he has said so. We believe him to be who he says he is, namely God; therefore, he is truth, and he has the power to accomplish this sublime miracle of love. For us who call ourselves Christians, lovers of Christ, the natural response to the doctrine of the Eucharist should be to go and spend time with Jesus. "Because Christ himself is present in the sacrament of the altar, he is to be honored with the worship of adoration. 'To visit the Blessed Sacrament is . . . a proof of gratitude, an expression of love, and a duty of adoration toward Christ Our Lord.'"[44] As was stated earlier, we become what we love. Therefore, love of the Blessed Sacrament will transform us into Christ. The prompt and wholehearted response of Bartimaeus to hearing that Jesus of Nazareth was present

---

[44] *Catechism of the Catholic Church,* 1418.

should be the normal response of those who believe in the eucharistic presence of Christ. There would be a serious disconnect between our head and our heart if we were to say that we love Christ, that we know that he is truly present in the Blessed Sacrament, and yet spend no time with him outside of the Sunday Mass obligation, or, for priests, outside of daily Mass. Love goes beyond obligation or it is not love at all, but only duty. We would not say that a married couple had a deeply loving relationship if they only did what they were obliged to do for each other and no more. Love is sacrificial.

Once Bartimaeus knows that Jesus is present, his entire "prayer" changes in form and orientation. The change in form is seen in the shift from begging, which represents superficial prayers of petition for personal material needs, to a cry for mercy. The change in orientation is seen in the shift from petitions thrown out to anyone who will hear him, to a cry directed toward Jesus himself. He refers to Christ specifically as "Son of David," which is to acknowledge that God has come in the flesh. The Lord has a real human nature, and it is through his human nature that we receive salvation. His human nature, in which the fullness of divinity dwells, is the source of all grace. That same body, blood, soul, and divinity are what we adore in the Blessed Sacrament. If we truly believe what we claim to believe regarding the real presence of Jesus in the Blessed Sacrament, then our prayer must grow and change in imitation of Bartimaeus. Our entire life should witness to the reality that Jesus Christ dwells among us! In every tabernacle and every monstrance throughout the world is the same Jesus who healed Bartimaeus, walked on water, raised the dead, cleansed lepers, calmed storms, revealed the face of the Father, and eventually suffered and died for love of us. That same power, that same beautiful face, and that same eternal love are waiting for us day and night in the Blessed Sacrament. Our love becomes rightly ordered when we love the Blessed Sacrament above all things and creatures. That is the beautiful truth that Tolkien conveyed to his son in one of his letters: "Out of the darkness of my life, so much frustrated, I put before you the one great thing to love on earth: the Blessed Sacrament. . . . There you will find romance, glory, honor, fidelity, and the true way of all your loves upon earth, and more than that: death: by the divine paradox, that which ends life, and demands the surrender of all, and yet by the taste (or foretaste) of which alone can what you seek in your earthly relationships (love, faithfulness, joy) be maintained, or take on that complexion of reality, of eternal endurance, which every man's heart desires."[45] Love of the Blessed Sacrament is love of God. "Whoever seeks to consult with the eucharistic God in all her concerns, whoever lets herself be purified by the sanctifying power coming from the sacrifice at the altar, offering herself to the Lord in this sacrifice, whoever receives the Lord in her soul's innermost depth in holy Communion cannot but be drawn ever more deeply and powerfully into the flow of divine life, incorporated into the mystical Body of Christ, her heart converted to the likeness of the divine heart."[46]

A Cry for Mercy

Mercy is the love of God as it is directed toward sinners. The prayer for mercy that Bartimaeus cries out in Christ's presence is the most perfect and necessary prayer. A true cry for mercy implicitly contains contrition, humility, the

---

[45] J. R. R. Tolkien, *The Letters of J. R. R. Tolkien: A Selection*, Kindle edition, loc. 1111-1115.

[46] Edith Stein, *Essays on Woman*, Kindle edition, loc. 936-939.

acknowledgement of sinfulness, and yet also trust in the love of God. It comes from the type of heart that should be the template for all hearts seeking to be heard by God. It is a humble and contrite heart that draws the merciful gaze of the Savior. "But this is the man to whom I will look, he that is humble and contrite in spirit, and trembles at my word" (Is 66:2). The gaze of Christ from the Blessed Sacrament has power to convert and sanctify us as it did the apostle Matthew.[47] "The encounter with him [Christ] is the decisive act of judgment. Before his gaze all falsehood melts away. This encounter with him, as it burns us, transforms and frees us, allowing us to become truly ourselves. All that we build during our lives can prove to be mere straw, pure bluster, and it collapses. Yet in the pain of this encounter, when the impurity and sickness of our lives become evident to us, there lies salvation. His gaze, the touch of his heart, heals us through an undeniably painful transformation 'as through fire.' But it is a blessed pain, in which the holy power of his love sears through us like a flame, enabling us to become totally ourselves and thus totally of God."[48]

---

[47] Matthew 9:9.

"Saint Ambrose: When you hide your face, all grows weak (Ps 104:29): if you turn to look at me, woe is me! You have nothing to see in me but the stain of my crimes; there is no gain either in being abandoned or in being seen, because when we are seen, we offend you. Still, we can imagine that God does not reject those he sees, because he purifies those upon whom he gazes. Before him burns a fire capable of consuming our guilt (cf. Joel 2:3)"[49]

> *For thus says the high and lofty One who inhabits eternity, whose name is holy: "I dwell in the high and holy place, and also with him who is of a contrite and humble spirit, to revive the spirit of the humble, and to revive the heart of the contrite" (Is 57:15).*

Bartimaeus doesn't just ask for mercy; he *cries* out for it! A cry is something that comes from the very depth of our being, welling up in the heart. Therefore, his prayer has changed, as we said, from monotonous begging to a heartfelt cry! The Greek verb used here by Mark to

---

[48] Pope Benedict XVI, Encyclical on Christian Hope *Spe Salvi* (30 November 2007), § 47.

[49] Pope John Paul II, Encyclical on the Splendour of Truth *Veritatis Splendor* (6 August 1993), § 105.

describe Bartimaeus crying out is exactly the same word used right before Jesus died: "And Jesus uttered a loud cry, and breathed his last" (Mk 15:37). In a certain sense, Bartimaeus is beginning to pray in a way that is mysteriously linked to the passion of Christ. This is true of any meritorious or efficacious prayer. All graces and merit come from the passion and death of Jesus. Any merit in our prayer is sourced in the sacrifice of Christ on Calvary. We are united with this sacrifice through the Mass and eucharistic adoration. The passion and death of Christ is the perfect prayer, the perfect sacrifice, not because it was the right amount of blood, but rather the right amount of love. The God of love died for our sakes on the cross, and it is from the depths of his eternal love that his final cry issues forth. When we pray in the presence of the Blessed Sacrament, our prayers are united to the prayers of Jesus, and they become a cry that moves the heart of the Father to mercy. In eucharistic adoration we place our prayers in the furnace of the Sacred Heart and they take on the infinite efficacy of the precious Blood. Every single holy hour we make dramatically changes the world for the better. In the presence of the Blessed Sacrament we begin to burn more intensely and love more ardently. Not only do we pray *with* him when we are in adoration, but we begin to pray *like* him. We leave behind our own desires and take on the desires of Christ. "Life with the eucharistic Savior induces the soul to be lifted out of the narrowness of its individual, personal orbit. The concerns of the Lord and his kingdom become the soul's concerns."[50]

Bartimaeus is also persevering in his cry for mercy. In a sense he is the echo of all the generations since the sin of Adam and Eve. He is the personification of fallen mankind. Original sin brought not only death but also the loss of the interior integrity of our souls. Our intellects lost the preternatural gift of infused knowledge, and they became darkened. Our wills lost the divine strength, and they became weak. Our passions are no longer subject to reason, and they cry out beyond due proportion within us. Bartimaeus's blindness represents the darkened intellect, that he is sitting down represents the weak will, and his begging represents the passions all crying out to be satisfied. And so, Bartimaeus represents all of us who suffer from the effects of original sin crying out for

---

[50] Edith Stein, *Essays on Woman*, Kindle edition, loc. 2056-2057.

interior healing from the Lord; that he will have mercy on us. Christ's response to this cry for mercy is so beautiful to contemplate. The passage says simply, "Jesus stopped and said, 'call him'" (Mk 10:49). So Jesus stops, and he speaks. One of the definitions for *abide* is "to linger in a place or to remain present." Therefore, by stopping, Jesus is simply abiding in a specific place and remaining present there. He is also speaking, or communicating, his word. Mercy is not something God has, but rather who God is. Mercy is one of his divine attributes, which means that God is mercy. Therefore, when we ask for mercy, God gives us himself. Jesus Christ, the word, gives himself to us through sacred scripture and the Eucharist. Christ's word and presence are his answer to humanity's cry for mercy. That is why the Mass is the fount of mercy, because it consists of the Liturgy of the Word and the Liturgy of the Eucharist. The Mass is where Jesus literally stops and speaks to us. But as Bishop Sheen says, "Liturgy is insufficient for total spirituality. Sometimes liturgy can be used as an excuse for a want of personal piety."[51] We cannot only pray the prayers that are obliged

---

[51] Fulton Sheen, *The Holy Hour and Fighting Evil*, Retreat on the Priesthood 1, 7 mins 41 secs audio, from FultonSheen.com

of us. The Mass especially must flow out and saturate our entire life. We should prolong and intensify our union with Christ in the Mass through daily eucharistic adoration and daily scriptural meditation. These two things prepare us for a deeper communion with Jesus, and they dispose us for a truly full and active participation in the Mass. Full active participation in the Mass is not measured by how much I do or contribute in the Mass through various ministries. It is not measured by how much I give, but how much I receive, and how disposed I am to receive. We all hear the same scripture during the Mass, but we don't all receive understanding of it to the same degree. We all, in grace and of age, receive the same Christ in holy Communion, but we don't all receive the same benefit from our holy Communions. The more we actively love scripture and the Blessed Sacrament, the more we will increase our full active participation in the Mass. The simplest and most effective way to actively love scripture is to set aside time for daily personal scriptural meditation. And in order to become better disposed for holy Communion, and thus benefit more by it, we should take up daily eucharistic adoration.

(Catholic MP3 Vault, 2011).

True Disciples

The Eucharist is the filter that proves those who are true, loving disciples of Christ. The Blessed Sacrament is Christ, and any time spent with him is an act of love for him. To be a disciple means to sit at the feet of the master, and we are formed into loving disciples through time spent in adoration sitting at the feet of our eucharistic King. True discipleship is proven based on our response to the Eucharist. It is the fire that proves those who desire to follow Christ. When John and Andrew asked the Lord where he dwelt, he said to them, "come and see."[52] The first thing the Lord required of his first two disciples was that they come to the place where he dwelt. They had to be disciples before they could be apostles. They had to abide with Jesus and spend time in his presence before they could be sent out. In John

---

[52] "The next day again John was standing with two of his disciples; and he looked at Jesus as he walked, and said, 'Behold, the Lamb of God!' The two disciples heard him say this, and they followed Jesus. Jesus turned, and saw them following, and said to them, 'What do you seek?' And they said to him, 'Rabbi' (which means Teacher), 'where are you staying?' He said to them, 'Come and see.' They came and saw where he was staying; and they stayed with him that day, for it was about the tenth hour. One of the two who heard John speak, and followed him, was Andrew, Simon Peter's brother" (Jn 1:35-40).

chapter 6, Jesus again separates his true disciples from false disciples through his teaching on the Eucharist. The Eucharist is the perpetuation of the Incarnation. The Eucharist is the presence of God with us. "Many left him" (v. 66), because they could not accept the teaching on the Eucharist. This represents those who call themselves disciples of Christ but deny the doctrine of the Real Presence, and therefore never draw close to the presence of Jesus in the Blessed Sacrament. While those who accept the eucharistic doctrine—those united with Peter—remain in the presence of Christ. The disciples who did not accept this teaching left his presence, because they were scandalized by the way in which the Lord desires to abide with us. Time spent in eucharistic adoration is a necessary requirement for those who wish to be disciples of Jesus Christ.

Bringing Christ to the World

When Moses would return to the Israelites after spending time in the presence of God there would be a lingering radiance shining out from his face.

> *When Moses came down from Mount Sinai, with the two tablets of the testimony in his hand as he came down*

from the mountain, Moses did not know that the skin of his face shone because he had been talking with God. And when Aaron and all the people of Israel saw Moses, behold, the skin of his face shone, and they were afraid to come near him. But Moses called to them; and Aaron and all the leaders of the congregation returned to him, and Moses talked with them. And afterward all the people of Israel came near, and he gave them in commandment all that the Lord had spoken with him on Mount Sinai. And when Moses had finished speaking with them, he put a veil on his face; but whenever Moses went in before the Lord to speak with him, he took the veil off, until he came out; and when he came out, and told the people of Israel what he was commanded, the people of Israel saw the face of Moses, that the skin of Moses' face shone; and Moses would put the veil upon his face again, until he went in to speak with him (Ex 34:29-35).

This is the model of life for all priests. "The Eucharist is the principal and central raison d'être of the sacrament of the priesthood . . . The priest fulfills his principal mission and is manifested in all his fullness when he celebrates the Eucharist, and this manifestation is more complete when he himself allows the depth of that mystery to become visible, so that it alone shines forth in people's hearts and minds, through his ministry. This is the supreme exercise of the 'kingly priesthood,' 'the source and summit of all Christian life.'"[53] When a priest spends time with Jesus in adoration every day, it shines out from his face. He speaks with greater authority because of the conviction that comes from time spent with the Lord. The face of Jesus Christ becomes more reflected in his face with each holy hour.[54] However, this is not just for priests; we are all called to bring Christ to the world. How can we do that without spending time with him? "Eucharistic worship constitutes the soul of all Christian life. In fact, Christian life is expressed in the fulfilling of the greatest commandment, that is to say, in

[53] Pope John Paul II, Letter on the Mystery and Worship of the Eucharist *Dominicae Cenae* (24 February 1980), § 2.

[54] "Before the people could believe in us, there had to be about our brow something of the sheen of Moses' halo when he came down from Sinai and approached the children of Israel. In the eyes of the Hebrew people, this halo bore witness to the intimacy of God's ambassador with the One by whom he was sent. And the success of our own mission demanded not only that we be known as men of honor and conviction, but also a ray of glory from the Eucharist, to give to the people some intimation of the living God, whom none can resist." Chautard, *Soul of the Apostolate*, Kindle edition, 192.

the love of God and neighbor, and this love finds its source in the Blessed Sacrament, which is commonly called the sacrament of love."[55] We most truly bring Christ to the world when we make the Eucharist more known and loved. Our faces should shine with the joy that comes from gazing through the eyes of faith upon the beautiful face of Jesus. Saint Pius X called the Church to "'reestablish all things in Christ.' It summarizes the program of an apostle who lives on the Eucharist and who sees that the Church will gain successes only in proportion as souls make progress in the eucharistic life."[56]

Is adoration difficult? It can be for a time, but with perseverance it becomes pure sweetness. This perseverance increases our faith, and it is faith that the Lord holds so dear to his sacred heart. He looks out from the monstrance with tender love upon the adorer there before him, who is there because of faith. Even though we do not see, we believe. "In this you rejoice, though now for a little while you may have to suffer various trials, so that the genuineness of your faith, more precious than

---

[55] *Dominicae Cenae,* § 5.

[56] Chautard, *Soul of the Apostolate,* Kindle edition, 189-190.

gold which though perishable is tested by fire, may redound to praise and glory and honor at the revelation of Jesus Christ. *Without having seen him you love him; though you do not now see him you believe in him* and rejoice with unutterable and exalted joy. As the outcome of your faith you obtain the salvation of your souls (emphasis added)" (1 Pt 1:6-9).

Adoration Will Change the World

The Lord is veiled in the Eucharist, so that we can learn to love him for himself, and not for his gifts or consolations. He is a king who disguises himself in order to see if he is truly loved for his own sake and not because of his wealth. To love or desire anything above the Blessed Sacrament reveals a disorder, and it is something that must be purified out of the soul. In the Eucharist our hearts are satisfied, because in the Eucharist we find the beloved. "Every earthly affection, even that which seems to be the deepest, is superficial. Our hearts were not made for created things, although these things attract us inasmuch as they are reflections of the divine. But they neither satisfy nor pacify human hearts, nor produce in them the interior movement proper to profound love, the love of God. If men really knew what love is! If they knew that after years spent in devoting to creatures what they think is a deep and wonderful love, they are still ignorant of the first rudiments of the divine science. They have not even begun to taste the holy delights of a love so profound that it touches the roots of our being, so great that it fills the immense emptiness of our souls, so ardent that it carries us out of ourselves, so sweet that it enraptures us, so strong that it transforms us, so lasting that it is immortal! No love equals the love of the soul that has had a glimpse of God in the midst of the gloom of earth. For this fortunate soul has not found love, but Love."[57]

Jesus, the beloved, is also veiled in the Eucharist so that we will grow in the perfection of the theological virtues of faith, hope, and charity. These are the highest virtues because they are the virtues that unite us to God. They have God as their object. The highest act of faith for us is an act of faith in the Eucharist, which is the source and summit of our faith. The highest act of hope for us is an act of hope in the Eucharist, which contains

---

[57] Luis M. Martínez, *The Sanctifier*, 335.

him whom we hope to possess for eternity. The highest act of love for us is an act of love for the Eucharist, because love himself is the direct recipient of that act. Every instant we are before the Lord in eucharistic adoration, by simply being there, we are exercising the highest acts of faith, hope, and love. This is why we should persevere in adoration, especially through dark and dry times in prayer, because this only serves to increases our faith, hope, and love. Eucharistic adoration is the school where we learn and grow in these virtues. As we see with Bartimaeus, it is his perseverance in prayer with faith that leads him to draw near to Christ and receive complete healing. This journey is difficult and many obstacles appear to prevent a soul's movement toward Christ. When Bartimaeus begins to pray for mercy he is rebuked by the multitude: "And many rebuked him, telling him to be silent; but he cried out all the more, 'Son of David, have mercy on me!'" (Mk 10:48). This is what must be expected when we begin to draw near to Christ—there will be a multitude attempting to stop us.[58]

Eucharistic adoration is what will change the world.

---

[58] "My son, if you come forward to serve the Lord, prepare yourself for trials" (Sir 2:1).

It is the triumph of the immaculate heart of Mary, who desires only that her Son is known and loved. The world today is infected with sin and darkness to a greater extent than ever before. Yet, where sin abounds, grace abounds all the more.[59] "Infection from the ills of former ages could well enough be countered, and souls preserved in health, by a merely ordinary piety. But the virulence of the pestilence in our own times, a hundred times more deadly and so quickly caught from the fatal attractions of the world, must be fought with a much more powerful serum."[60] The serum needed for souls today is a deeply eucharistic life of Communion and adoration. In the Lord's battle against the hour of darkness and sin, he asked his disciples for an hour of adoration: "Could you not watch one hour with me?"[61] It is reasonable to think that the Lord prayed for about three hours in Gethsemane, if we go by the accounts in Matthew and

---

[59] Romans 5:20.

[60] Chautard, *Soul of the Apostolate*, Kindle edition, 190.

[61] "Then he said to them, 'My soul is very sorrowful, even to death; remain here, and watch with me.' And he came to the disciples and found them sleeping; and he said to Peter, 'So, could you not watch with me one hour?'" (Mt 26:38, 40).

Mark.[62] Before he began, he asked his disciples to remain there and to keep watch with him. So when he comes and finds them sleeping, he rebukes them for not being able to watch even one hour. One hour is thus a minimum, not a maximum! It is an obligation, not just a nice thing to do. The Greek word for "remain here" is *meno*. It means to abide or to remain present. Jesus means for them to remain present where he is present, to abide where he abides. The word used for the distance that Jesus moved forward from them is *mikron*. It's where we get the word micron—a micrometer. That is the closeness we have to Christ in adoration—he is so very near to us. Saint Luke gives a mysterious measure for this distance, which seems to be an analogy for linking Christ to King David. King David, when he was fleeing from his son who was trying to kill him, was walking up the Mount of Olives weeping. Once David passed the summit of the Mount of Olives, he arrived at Bahurim and was pelted with stones by Shime-i.[63] Therefore, it is very significant when Luke tells us, "And he [Jesus] withdrew from them

---

[62] Matthew 26:36-46 and Mark 14:32-42.

[63] 2 Samuel 16:5-7, 11-13.

about a stone's throw, and knelt down and prayed"
(22:41). Those guilty of certain sins were stoned to death.
And so Christ, who is now taking all the guilt of our sins
upon himself, is placing himself on the receiving end of
that punishment. Like King David, once Jesus passed the
summit of the Mount of Olives, his passion began. It was
David's own flesh and blood that is seeking to kill him.
For the Lord, it was those to whom he had given his flesh
and blood who would betray and abandon him. It was his
priests.

Resisting the Multitude

In response to such love from the Lord, an hour in his
presence is the least we can do, besides being the means
that Christ gives us to fight the darkness of sin and evil.
"The Church and the world have a great need of
eucharistic worship Jesus waits for us in this sacrament
of love. Let us be generous with our time in going to
meet him in adoration and in contemplation that is full of
faith and ready to make reparation for the great faults and
crimes of the world."[64] In eucharistic adoration, we take

---

[64] Dominicae Cenae, § 3.

Christ, the light of the world, and we place him on the lampstand, which is the altar.[65] The Eucharist is the light in the darkness. "The light shines in the darkness, and the darkness has not overcome it" (Jn 1:5). The darkness has not, and will not, overcome the light. It hurls itself instead against those who seek the light. The same multitude—at least the spirit behind it—that tried to stop Bartimaeus seeking Christ and crying out for mercy is the spirit that hurls itself as a multitude against all those who seek Christ and his mercy today.

The Greek word for multitude is *polus* (pol-oos). It means many, much, or large. This multitude, which tries to stop us coming to Christ and his mercy in adoration, can be both exterior or interior, as well as spiritual or material. The multitude can be all the many exterior attractions of the world. It is also the noise of today, which drowns out consciences, erasing the silence necessary to truly face ourselves and the deeper questions about life and meaning. Bishop Fulton Sheen said, "The holy hour in our modern rat race is necessary for authentic prayer. Our world is one of speed in which

---

[65] "And he said to them, 'Is a lamp brought in to be put under a bushel, or under a bed, and not on a stand?'" (Mk 4:21).

intensity of movement is a substitute for lack of purpose; where noise is invoked to drown out the whisperings of conscience; where talk, talk, talk gives the impression that we are doing something when really we are not; where activity kills self-knowledge won by contemplation . . ."[66] The multitude can also be the constant barrage of verbal attacks against eucharistic adoration by the so-called enlightened. The multitude might also be something interior. It may be the memory of past sins and a dissolute life that makes us think we are not worthy of drawing near to Christ himself in the Blessed Sacrament. It might be all of the distractions and useless thoughts that come when we try to pray and make us think that we will never be able to pray deeply. The multitude may be all of the sinful inclinations and desires that we think we need to be rid of before we come to Jesus in adoration. Jesus is the One who makes us holy; we don't get holy and then come to Jesus. The multitude can also be temptations to do other good things, instead of focusing on the greatest good, which is the Eucharist. This can be

---

[66] This quote is widely attributed to Bishop Sheen. While not being able to locate this exact statement in his talks and writings, it is at least a true paraphrase of his thoughts on the holy hour as necessity for genuine prayer and a remedy against activism.

other programs, ministries—even parish activities and outreaches. These are good in themselves but should not replace time with Jesus. If we are too busy for eucharistic adoration, we are too busy! Especially priests. If we could replace all of the hours spent in front of the television, computers, and on social media with holy hours of adoration, the Church militant would be holy, and holiness is what is needed to convert the culture. Pope Benedict XVI said that "the secret of their [priests'] sanctification lies precisely in the Eucharist. . . . The priest must be first and foremost an adorer who contemplates the Eucharist."[67] When we behold the Lord in adoration, our soul increases from glory to glory.[68] However, it is not only ourselves who are sanctified though our time spent in adoration but also the entire world.[69] This is why

---

[67] Pope Benedict XVI, Angelus, 18 September 2005.

[68] "And we all, with unveiled face, beholding the glory of the Lord, are being changed into his likeness from one degree of glory to another; for this comes from the Lord who is the Spirit" (2 Cor 3:18).

[69] "Through adoration, the Christian mysteriously contributes to the radical transformation of the world and to the sowing of the Gospel. Anyone who prays to the Savior draws the whole world with him and raises it to God. Those who stand before the Lord are therefore fulfilling an eminent service. They are presenting to

we must persevere like Bartimaeus against the multitude. We must cry out all the more in the presence of the eucharistic King: "Son of David, have mercy on me!" (Mk 10:48). This is essentially the battle of prayer, the battle against the multitude in the loving pursuit of the One.

The tactic of the spirit of the multitude is to rebuke us as it did Bartimaeus. The Greek word for rebuke is e*pitimao*. It means "to raise the price of" or "to tax." The devil tempts us, as we said in the previous chapter, to think that mercy is beyond our reach, or in a certain sense out of our price range. Now this contains some truth—as all temptations and heresies do—but not the whole truth. While *we* cannot pay for mercy, Christ has obtained mercy for us. He has paid for it with his life. He is mercy, and he gives himself to us in the Eucharist. "For every Catholic there lies ready an immeasurable treasure: the proximity of the Lord in the holy sacrifice and in the most holy sacrament of the altar. Whoever is imbued with a lively faith in Christ present in the tabernacle, whoever knows

Christ all those who do not know him or are far from him: they keep watch in his presence on their behalf." Pope John Paul II, Letter to the Bishop of Liege on the 750th Anniversary of the feast of Corpus Christi (28 May 1996), § 5, at catholicsaints.info/pope-john-paul-ii-letter-on-the-750th-anniversary-of-the-feast-of-corpus-christi-28-may-1996/ (accessed 24 May 2017).

that a friend awaits here constantly—always with the time, patience, and sympathy to listen to complaints, petitions, and problems, with counsel and help in all things—this person cannot remain desolate and forsaken even under the greatest difficulties. He always has a refuge where quietude and peace can again be found."[70]

Adoration and Vocation

To this complete gift of Christ himself, love requires that we respond with a complete gift of ourselves. This is especially true for all those in religious life or the priesthood. Formation for both should require daily eucharistic adoration, or at least a daily holy hour. The fruits of eucharistic adoration are becoming more and more visible today. We meet an ever-increasing number of people—priests, religious, married couples—whose vocations were received through time spent with Christ in adoration. Many do not hear the vocational call today because of the cacophony that deafens us. To hear the call, it is necessary to spend time in silence with the One who calls. It would be a serious cause for concern if we were to go through the entire formation process, of either

[70] Edith Stein, *Essays on Woman*, Kindle edition, loc. 1972-1976.

seminary or religious formation, and not spend time each day with Christ in the Blessed Sacrament (outside of the required prayer times). If we take no personal time with Jesus, the relationship will never become personal. It would be tragic for a seminarian or religious to go through the entire formation process and know a lot *about* Jesus, but not know Jesus personally. Or, to know everything about the Church, and yet not love the eucharistic beating heart of the Church. If our relationship with Jesus is only theoretical, or only to the extent of fulfilling our obligations, then our vocation will falter and we will lack the fire necessary to convert souls. If, however, we put theory into practice, turn knowledge into love, and incorporate eucharistic adoration into our daily lives, then our hearts will be set ablaze and we will receive power from on high to evangelize with abundant fruitfulness. In addition to this we can receive great consolation from the words of Bishop Fulton Sheen, which could be applied to every vocation: "No priest will ever be lost who makes the daily holy hour."[71]

---

[71] Fulton Sheen, *Reflecting Christ in the Society*, Retreat on the Priesthood 1, 24 mins 33 secs audio, from FultonSheen.com (Catholic MP3 Vault, 2011).

Jesus said, "I came to cast fire upon the earth; and would that it were already kindled!" (Lk 12:49). It is in the Gospel of John chapter 21 where we find the only fire ever kindled by Jesus himself in scripture. When the disciples arrive on land, it says that "they saw a charcoal fire laid down there, with fish lying on it, and bread" (Jn 21:9). *Keimai* is the verb used here to describe the fire as being "laid down." It is the same verb used when laying down a foundation, or establishing a throne. The Lord came to cast the fire of divine love upon the earth, to set this love as the foundation for our lives and to set up his throne of love. The gift that comes to us from that love is the Eucharist, represented by the fish and bread. The fish and bread represent the humanity of Christ, which he laid down in the loving sacrifice of himself for our sakes. There is no other pain like the pain of an all-consuming love that meets only with indifference. Jesus thirsts for us to return his love! He thirsts to the point where it consumes him.[72]

---

[72] Jesus spoke to Saint Margaret Mary Alacoque during an apparition in the octave leading up to the feast of Corpus Christi saying, "'Behold,' said he to her, 'this heart which has so loved men that it has spared nothing, even to exhausting and consuming itself, in order to testify its love. In return, I receive from the greater part only ingratitude, by their irreverence and sacrilege, and

It was the belief of Saint John Paul II that "it is not enough for Catholics to receive the Eucharist. One also must contemplate it." He said that when one ponders the love that is present in the tabernacle, ". . . love is ignited within us, love is renewed within us. Therefore, these are not hours spent in idleness, when we isolate ourselves from our work, but these are moments, hours, when we undertake something that constitutes the deepest meaning of all of our work. For no matter how numerous our activities, our ministries, however numerous our concerns, our exertions—if there is no love, everything becomes meaningless. When we devote our time to ponder the mystery of love, to allow it to radiate in our hearts, we are preparing ourselves in the best possible way for any kind of service, for any activity, for any charitable work."[73]

---

by the coldness and contempt they have for me in this sacrament of love. And what is most painful to me,' added the Savior, in a tone that went to the sister's heart, 'is that they are hearts consecrated to me.'" Emile Bougaud, *Revelations of the Sacred Heart to Blessed Margaret Mary and the History of Her Life* (New York: Benziger Brothers, 1890), Kindle edition, loc. 2697.

[73] Jason Evert, *Saint John Paul the Great: His Five Loves*, Kindle edition, loc. 1771.

Prayer to Be a Eucharistic Soul

I want to be a eucharistic soul, a hidden apostle of the divine heart. To practice complete, confident, and loving abandonment. To go to God by means of the cross, through the heart of Jesus, under the sweet maternal protection of Mary. Whatever it may be, let the future be welcome, since it comes from the heavenly Father and the one Friend. As the future becomes the present, it will bring me its own necessary graces. Until then and even afterward I must remember that "sufficient unto the day is the evil thereof" and that the present day is the one during which I can work and suffer for souls, for the glory of God.[74]

---

[74] Elisabeth Leseur, *Secret Diary of Elisabeth Leseur* (Manchester, New Hampshire: Sophia Institute Press, 2012), Kindle edition, loc. 2163-2168.

THE FOURTH PRINCIPLE:
IMMERSION IN THE MYSTERIES OF CHRIST THROUGH THE GOSPELS AND THE ROSARY

———————— ● ————————

And Jesus stopped and said, "Call him." And they called the blind man, saying to him, "Take heart; rise, he is calling you." And throwing off his mantle he sprang up and came to Jesus (Mk 10:49-50).

The inspired Word, meaning scripture, when properly interpreted and understood will always lead us to the natural Word where he is present in the Eucharist. Scripture leads us to Christ, and thus, our relationship and closeness to the Blessed Sacrament is the indicator of how well we have understood scripture and have lived by it. "Word and Eucharist are so deeply bound together that we cannot understand one without the other: the Word of God sacramentally takes flesh in the event of the Eucharist. The Eucharist opens us to an understanding of scripture, just as scripture for its part illumines and explains the mystery of the Eucharist. Unless we acknowledge the Lord's real presence in the Eucharist, our understanding of scripture remains imperfect."[75] Therefore we should never go to our holy hours without our bible or a good Catholic bible commentary.[76] "All must imitate their divine Model, and in order to do this they must meditate on the mysteries of his life, of his virtues, and of his glory. It is a great mistake to think that only priests and religious and those who have withdrawn from the turmoil of the world are supposed to meditate upon the truths of our faith and the mysteries of the life of Christ. If priests and religious have an obligation to

---

[75] Pope Benedict XVI, Post-Synodal Apostolic Exhortation on the Word of God in the Life and Mission of the Church *Verbum Domini* (30 September, 2010), § 55.

[76] Some examples of what to use: *Catena Aurea*; the *Commentaries* of St. Thomas Aquinas, St. Augustine, or St. John Chrysostom on the gospels; *The Ignatius Press Study Bible*; *The Navarre Bible* series.

meditate on the great truths of our holy religion in order to live up to their vocation worthily, the same obligation is just as much incumbent on the laity, because of the fact that every day they meet with spiritual dangers which might cause them to lose their souls."[77]

The best place for scriptural meditation is in the presence of the Blessed Sacrament. While we can perform our daily prayer and scriptural meditation anywhere, and merit by it, there is a hierarchy of places in which to pray. The Lord is present *par excellence* in the Blessed Sacrament, which makes it the best location in which to pray because it is the place where we are most truly at his feet. "Saint Francis of Assisi: 'Prayer is the source of grace. Preaching is the channel that pours out the graces we ourselves have received from heaven. The ministers of the Word of God have been chosen by the great King to carry to the people of the earth what they themselves have learned and gathered from his lips, especially before the tabernacle.'"[78] The lamp that enlightens scripture is the Eucharist because it is the Lord who teaches us. "In thy light do we

---

[77] Saint Louis Marie de Montfort, *The Secret of the Rosary* (2013), Kindle edition, loc. 902-906.

[78] Chautard, *Soul of the Apostolate*, Kindle edition, 194.

see light" (Ps 36:9). The Eucharist sheds light on scripture. As we read in the Book of Revelation chapter 5, it is the lamb who was slain who alone is worthy to open the seven seals of the scroll. Scripture is only perfectly, or fully, revealed in the light of the lamb who was slain, which is Jesus in the Eucharist. In turn, a deeper understanding of scripture, as it is fulfilled in Christ (and therefore fulfilled in the Eucharist), sets our hearts on fire and causes an increased recognition of Jesus in the *breaking of the bread*.[79] "A faith-filled understanding of sacred scripture must always refer back to the liturgy."[80] "Saint Jerome famously said: 'Ignorance of scripture is ignorance of Christ.' It is equally true that ignorance of Christ—Christ really present in the Eucharist—is ignorance of scripture."[81] Almost all of the post-Resurrection encounters with Christ in the gospels highlight that it is through the Word that we arrive at a

---

[79] Lk 24:30-32.

[80] *Verbum Domini*, § 52.2.

[81] Scott Hahn, *Consuming the Word: The New Testament and the Eucharist in the Early Church* (New York: The Doubleday Religious Publishing Group, 2013), Kindle edition, loc. 1671-1673.

deeper appreciation and recognition of Christ's presence. The general theme of the post-Resurrection encounters is the following: firstly, Christ makes himself present but is unrecognizable to the senses. Secondly, he speaks and enters into conversation with them. Lastly, there is the recognition of the Lord as manifest by John's "it is the Lord," (Jn 21:7) or Magdalene's "rabboni," (Jn 20:16) or the disciples on the road to Emmaus who recognize him "in the breaking of the bread" (Lk 24:35). This is true in the John chapter 21 account of the disciples who encounter the risen Lord on the shore of the lake after they have been fishing all night. These are the same criteria present in Luke's gospel for the disciples on the road to Emmaus.[82] The same is true for Mary Magdalene encountering Jesus at the tomb. He is first present but unrecognizable, then he speaks and causes them to

---

[82] "The Gospel of Luke relates that 'their eyes were opened and they recognized him' (24:31) only when Jesus took the bread, said the blessing, broke it, and gave it to them, whereas earlier 'their eyes were kept from recognizing him' (24:16). The presence of Jesus, first with his words and then with the act of breaking bread, made it possible for the disciples to recognize him. Now they were able to appreciate in a new way all that they had previously experienced with him: 'Did not our hearts burn within us while he talked to us on the road, while he opened to us the scriptures?' (24:32)." Pope Benedict XVI, *Verbum Domini*, § 54.2.

recognize that he is truly with them in the flesh. We need to spend time with scripture in order to recognize Christ in the Eucharist, a recognition that will hopefully manifest itself in the same radical responses that we see in the gospels. We need souls today with the same beautiful response of Peter, who leaps from the boat as soon as he recognizes the Lord so as to not waste a single second in getting to the feet of the One he loves.[83] We need souls like that of Mary Magdalene, who once recognizing the Teacher desire to cling to him and never let him go.[84] We need souls who desire to linger in the presence of Jesus, like the disciples in Emmaus who ask the Lord to remain with them because it was getting late.[85]

Effects of the Living Word

Bishop Fulton Sheen was right when he said numerous times that the Church is suffering from what he called a "de-Eucharistization." We have unfortunately all experienced this as true. We have seen men taking the

---

[83] Jn 21:7

[84] Jn 20:17

[85] Lk 24:29

place of God, when presiders' chairs replace the tabernacle at the center of many parishes. Sometimes tabernacles are removed altogether, and the Lord is banished from his own house. The way in which the Blessed Sacrament is treated and distributed in some places is heartbreaking. Vessels are not purified properly and particles of the sacred host are dropped and trampled upon. In some places where Communion is given under both species, the precious Blood is poured down the sacrarium after Mass instead of being consumed by the priest.[86] Sacrilege of this type is horrifically all too

---

[86] "'one who throws away the consecrated species or takes them away or keeps them for a sacrilegious purpose incurs a *latae sententiae* excommunication reserved to the Apostolic See; a cleric, moreover, may be punished by another penalty, not excluding dismissal from the clerical state.' To be regarded as pertaining to this case is any action that is voluntarily and gravely disrespectful of the sacred species. Anyone, therefore, who acts contrary to these norms, for example casting the sacred species into the sacrarium or in an unworthy place or on the ground, incurs the penalties laid down. Furthermore all will remember that once the distribution of holy Communion during the celebration of Mass has been completed, the prescriptions of the Roman Missal are to be observed, and in particular, whatever may remain of the Blood of Christ must be entirely and immediately consumed by the priest or by another minister, according to the norms, while the consecrated hosts that are left are to be consumed by the priest at the altar or carried to the place for the reservation of the Eucharist." Congregation for Divine Worship and the Discipline of the Sacrament on Certain Matters to be Observed or to be avoided regarding the Most Holy Eucharist *Redemptionis Sacramentum*,

common. Added to this is the lack of preaching on confession and the availability of some priests for the sacrament. We even hear of places where confession has been done away with as something "we don't do anymore." And so in a world where confessions are declining but sin is increasing, we have the added problem of sacrilegious Communions. We are in desperate need of a *re-Eucharistization* of the Church. We need an increased recognition of Jesus in the Blessed Sacrament through restoration to grace, consecration to Mary, and also through daily scriptural meditation. The Word of God purifies and cleanses us interiorly. "You are already made clean by the word which I have spoken to you" (Jn 15:3). The Word purifies our hearts, and it is only a pure heart that can see God.[87] "Read and ponder holy things; for the Word of God is pure, and it will make those pure who study it."[88] We need his living word to enlighten the darkness of our minds and hearts in order that we may truly see Jesus in the Eucharist. We need his

(23 April 2004), § 107.

[87] "Blessed are the pure in heart, for they shall see God" (Mt 5:8).

[88] Francis of Sales, *Introduction to the Devout Life - Enhanced Version*, Kindle edition, loc. 2119-2120.

"living and active" word to cause us to throw everything else aside and run to his presence.[89] It is this effect of the living Word that we see in the line from the healing of Bartimaeus at the beginning of the chapter.

When Jesus stops, he says, "Call him." Why does Jesus not just call Bartimaeus directly? Why does Jesus communicate his words to Bartimaeus through others? "And they called the blind man, saying to him, 'Take heart; rise, he is calling you'" (Mk 10:49). Well, just as Bartimaeus is the model for how we come to know of the presence of Christ, as mentioned above, he is also the model for how we receive the words of Christ, which is through others. This "they" who communicate the words of Jesus to Bartimaeus represent the gospel writers and the living voice of the Church for us. Jesus speaks, and they deliver his words. Therefore this "they" represents Christ speaking to us through scripture and tradition as interpreted through the magisterium of the Church.

The effect that this word has on Bartimaeus is then a beautiful example of what scriptural meditation, or an

---

[89] "For the word of God is living and active, sharper than any two-edged sword, piercing to the division of soul and spirit, of joints and marrow, and discerning the thoughts and intentions of the heart" (Heb 4:12).

inspired homily, should have upon us. To be clear, it is not just the reading of scripture but also the meditation upon and the contemplation of scripture that we are talking about. "When Jesus was upon earth 'virtue went out from him, and healed all': *Virtus de illo exibat et sanabat omnes*. Christ Jesus is ever the same; if with faith we contemplate his mysteries, either in the gospel or in the liturgy that the Church sets before us, the grace that he merited for us when he lived these mysteries is produced within us."[90] We need to take each word that we read and plant it in the rich soil of a soul that is in a state of grace. The Word will not grow in dead soil. Then we need to water each word with love, like Our Lady who "pondered all these things in her heart" (Lk 2:19). After some time a little sprout will appear from the soil; this sprout is the word or phrase that strikes us in the scene we are mediating upon. The more we look at the sprout, through the lens of our Catholic faith, watering it with loving contemplation, the more it grows. We should do this with each seed, each word, until it brings "forth grain, some a

---

[90] Columba Marmion, *Our Way and Our Life: Christ in His Mysteries*, abridged ed. (Tacoma, WA: Angelico Press, 2013), Kindle edition, loc. 122-124.

hundredfold, some sixty, some thirty. He who has ears, let him hear" (Mt 13:8-9). To read the Word without love, without sufficient time, or to be more anxious about the things of the world than the things of heaven, is to take the Word and scatter it on the rocky ground where it is picked up by birds, or on the pathway where it is trampled, or amid the thorns where it is choked.[91] So we must give love, time, and anxious concern to scripture in order for it to produce a rich harvest of virtue in our lives. In order for a priest's homily to be inspired, these same principles apply. Hearts will not be set on fire by the homilies of priests who have not been set ablaze themselves by the living Word.

Take Heart, Rise, He Is Calling You

The effects of this loving scriptural meditation are contained in the line addressed to Bartimaeus: "Take heart, rise, he is calling you"—a line composed of three

---

[91] "There are as many and varied methods of meditation as there are spiritual masters. Christians owe it to themselves to develop the desire to meditate regularly, lest they come to resemble the three first kinds of soil in the parable of the sower. But a method is only a guide; the important thing is to advance, with the Holy Spirit, along the one way of prayer: Christ Jesus." *Catechism of the Catholic Church*, 2707.

verbs in the Greek. Scripture gives us strength to do what we cannot; it gives us courage, causes us to rise up, and draws us to the presence of Christ.

Take heart. The Greek word used here for "take heart" is *tharseo*, which means "to be of good courage." Scripture dispels fear from our hearts. In the face of what appear to be insurmountable obstacles or trials, scripture gives us wisdom to see things from God's perspective. Then, when we look at anything through the eyes of God, the impossible becomes possible, and the insurmountable obstacles are uprooted and cast into the sea. Through scriptural meditation the virtues of Christ are also communicated to us. We increase in the virtues that we witness in the life of Christ when we lovingly meditate upon them. Our weak, fearful hearts become like the heart of the Lion of the tribe of Judah! The entire universe was created by the Word, and it is that same living Word that enlightens us and recreates us through scripture. The Word dispels the darkness, and with the darkness, our fear. We are created for the contemplation of God and the life of Christ. "And this is eternal life, that they know thee the only true God, and Jesus Christ whom thou hast sent" (Jn 17:3). The misuse of this capacity in us leads to anxiety, depression, despair, and a wide array of interior sufferings. When we give our time completely to the contemplation of evil in the world, the actions of men, politics, the news, etc., we lose perspective and hope. The horizon of the future grows dark and anxiety creeps in. When we give our minds over to the contemplation of the life of Christ, we are no longer surprised by the state of the world, we are not discouraged by the attacks against the Church or by the sinful actions of its members, because we have seen it all in his life, and we have learned and acquired the virtues to stand firm. In his life we recognize all the evils of our time present there too, but we also receive the power of the One contained in the pages we read. Those who are immersed in scripture radiate a peace that comes from knowing that all these things are taking place just as the Lord said they would. We rejoice that we are being treated like Christ and suffering for the sake of his name. We have courage, with the sword of his word, to stand up to the evil and darkness that surrounds us.

Rise up. The Greek word used here is *egeiro* (eg-i-ro), which is a verb meaning "to stand up, to wake up, to cause to exist, or to raise to life." We truly see here the great power of scripture when it is interiorized through meditation and contemplation, in the light of Church teaching and the early Fathers of the Church. Scripture communicates to us interior light and strength. Scripture causes our sleeping or dull intellects to wake up. Waking up is always associated with the opening of our eyes, and so scripture causes our intellects to *wake up* from the wisdom of men to the revelation of God, and thus the eyes of faith are opened within us. "So faith comes from what is heard, and what is heard comes by the preaching of Christ" (Rom 10:17). Scripture causes our weak wills, too feeble to stand for truth on their own, to stand up. It is not enough to know the truth; we must love the truth and act upon it. We must allow the Word to accomplish all things in us; we must say like Mary: "Be it done unto me according to thy word" (Lk 1:38). We are also interiorly recreated by means of scripture. The One who creates by his word also recreates by his word. The loving contemplation of the Lord and his life in the gospels enlightens our intellects, strengthens our wills, and orders our passions. His word also raises the dead back to life, through Baptism and absolution. His word, when it is cried out in the wilderness, calls sinners to repent so as to be brought from death to life. His words are what raise us from death to life, from darkness to light, from sadness to joy and from weakness to strength. However, in order for his words to have this effect in us, they must be not only read but also consumed, not only seen but also believed, and not only tasted but also devoured. "Thy words were found, and I ate them, and thy words became to me a joy and the delight of my heart; for I am called by thy name, O Lord, God of hosts" (Jer 15:16). "The knowledge of Jesus and of the various stages of his life is to be gained first of all from the gospels. It is enough for us to read these sacred pages so simple and so sublime—that is to say if we read them with faith—in order to see and hear Christ himself. For this book is inspired. Light and power go out from it to enlighten and strengthen souls that are upright and sincere. Happy are they who open it every day! They drink at the very wellspring of living waters."[92]

He is calling you. The Greek word used here is *phoneo*, which is a verb meaning "to call." The Lord speaks in order to draw us to himself. The scriptures draw us to Christ, to where the word himself is truly present, body,

---

[92] Columba Marmion, *Our Way and Our Life: Christ in His Mysteries*, Kindle edition, loc. 74-78.

blood, soul, and divinity. The life of Christ is also the model to which we should conform our lives. In the dark night of faith, scripture is the light that guides us. "Thy word is a lamp to my feet and a light to my path" (Ps 119:105). In confusion and darkness, it is the Word that gives us direction and light. His word leads us in our decisions and gives us confidence to persevere. "And your ears shall hear a word behind you, saying, 'This is the way, walk in it,' when you turn to the right or when you turn to the left" (Is 30:21). The line says, though: "Rise, he is calling *you*." Loving contemplation of scripture, especially the gospels, in the light of faith and through the eyes of the Church, causes conviction in us as to the personal call of Christ. We become convinced that he is not just calling *all* men to himself—he is calling *me*!

What we receive in meditation and contemplation is sweet in the mouth but bitter in the stomach. Truth received in prayer is sweet, but it is through bitterness and effort that these truths must be assimilated and digested into our lives. "So I went to the angel and told him to give me the little scroll; and he said to me, 'Take it and eat; it will be bitter to your stomach, but sweet as honey in your mouth.' And I took the little scroll from the hand of the angel and ate it; it was sweet as honey in my mouth, but when I had eaten it my stomach was made bitter" (Rv 10:9-10). We must respond to the Word as it convicts us of our sins and shows us how we ought to live and love. "Therefore put away all filthiness and rank growth of wickedness and receive with meekness the implanted word, which is able to save your souls. But be doers of the word, and not hearers only, deceiving yourselves. For if anyone is a hearer of the word and not a doer, he is like a man who observes his natural face in a mirror; for he observes himself and goes away and at once forgets what he was like. But he who looks into the perfect law, the law of liberty, and perseveres, being no hearer that forgets but a doer that acts, he shall be blessed in his doing" (Jas 1:21-25).

This is how we see Bartimaeus respond to the word he has received, and we should imitate his prompt example. He cooperates with the grace and virtue that are communicated to him through the words of Jesus as they are delivered to him. The words give him courage, and he throws away his mantle on which he relied for protection from the elements. He rids himself of all earthly comforts and seeks consolation and comfort in Christ alone. The words tell him to "rise," and so he springs up. They say "he is calling you," and so he responds and goes immediately to the feet of Christ. In that, we see that the final end of scripture is to lead us to the feet of Jesus in the Eucharist, because no one comes to the Father but by the Son. "Jesus said to him, 'I am the way, and the truth, and the life; no one comes to the Father but by me'" (Jn 14:6). The words of Jesus are not left dormant in Bartimaeus; he immediately acts upon them, cooperating with the virtue and grace he has received through them. Daily scriptural meditation, in the light of the faith, is a necessary requirement for those seeking perfection. It is not about intellectual capacity or abilities, nor about how strong or weak we are, but with the Church always as our interpreter, and through the eyes of faith, we are all called to dive in and immerse ourselves daily in sacred scripture. Holy scripture is a river in which the elephant may swim and the lamb may wade.[93] Let us take the following advice of Saint Francis de Sales and apply it to our daily

---

[93] "It is, as it were, a kind of river, if I may so liken it, which is both shallow [*planus*] and deep, wherein both the lamb may find a footing, and the elephant float at large." Saint Gregory the Great, *Morals on the Book of Job*, ed. Paul A Boer Sr. (London: Veritatis Splendor Publications, 2012), Kindle edition, loc. 1403.

lives:

> *But especially I commend earnest mental prayer to you, more particularly such as bears upon the life and passion of Our Lord. If you contemplate him frequently in meditation, your whole soul will be filled with him, you will grow in his likeness, and your actions will be molded on his. He is the light of the world; therefore in him, by him, and for him we shall be enlightened and illuminated; he is the tree of life, beneath the shadow of which we must find rest;—he is the living fountain of Jacob's well, wherein we may wash away every stain. Children learn to speak by hearing their mother talk, and stammering forth their childish sounds in imitation; and so if we cleave to the Savior in meditation, listening to his words, watching his actions and intentions, we shall learn in time, through his grace, to speak, act, and will like himself.[94]*

The Rosary as Scriptural Meditation

The Rosary is also a daily necessity and, since its mysteries ponder the events of Christ's life as told to us in scripture,

---

[94] Francis of Sales, *Introduction to the Devout Life - Enhanced Version*, Kindle edition, loc. 840-850.

is tied to our daily scriptural meditation. "Far from making you lose ground in mental prayer or stunting your spiritual growth, [the Rosary] will be a wonderful help to you. You will find it a real Jacob's ladder with fifteen rungs by which you will go from virtue to virtue and from light to light. Thus, without danger of being misled, you will easily arrive at the fullness of the age of Jesus Christ."[95] As we said above, Mary is the gateway into the mysteries of her Son. Through the Rosary, Mary takes our hand and teaches us how to ponder the mysteries of the life and passion of Jesus Christ in our hearts and to draw nourishment from them. "Far from being insignificant, the Rosary is a priceless treasure which is inspired by God. Almighty God has given it to you because he wants you to use it as a means to convert the most hardened sinners and the most obstinate heretics. He has attached to it grace in this life and glory in the next. The saints have said it faithfully and the popes have endorsed it. When the Holy Ghost has revealed this secret to a priest and director of souls, how blessed is that priest! For the vast majority of people fail to know this secret or else

---

[95] Saint Louis Marie de Montfort, *The Secret of the Rosary*, Kindle edition, loc. 940-943.

only know it superficially. If such a priest really understands this secret, he will say the Rosary each day and will encourage others to say it. God and his blessed Mother will pour abundant grace into his soul, so that he may become God's instrument for his glory; and his word, though simple, will do more good in one month than that of other preachers in several years."[96]

"Even if you are on the brink of damnation, even if you have one foot in hell, even if you have sold your soul to the devil as sorcerers do who practice black magic, and even if you are a heretic as obstinate as a devil, sooner or later you will be converted and will amend your life and save your soul, if—and mark well what I say—if you say the Rosary devoutly every day until death for the purpose of knowing the truth and obtaining contrition and pardon for your sins.[97] For never will anyone who says his Rosary every day become a formal heretic or be led astray by the devil. This is a statement which I would sign with my blood."[98]

---

[96] Ibid., Kindle edition, loc. 186-192.

[97] Ibid., Kindle edition, loc. 219-222.

[98] Ibid., Kindle edition, loc. 936-937.

THE FIFTH PRINCIPLE:
MASS AND HOLY COMMUNION

———————— • ————————

And throwing off his mantle he sprang up and came to Jesus. And Jesus said to him, 'What do you want me to do for you?' And the blind man said to him, 'Master, let me receive my sight.' And Jesus said to him, 'Go your way; your faith has made you well.' And immediately he received his sight and followed him on the way (Mk 10:50-52).

Lastly, we arrive at the Mass and our participation in the greatest and most perfect prayer of Christ. We arrive at the sacrifice that gives us the sacrament of the Body and Blood of Jesus Christ, allowing us to enter into the unfathomable intimacy of holy Communion with our benign king. The moment of holy Communion is the mountaintop of our earthly lives. It is the pinnacle to which we should always have the eyes of our hearts fixed. Our entire life should become a preparation for Communion, followed by a thanksgiving for having been counted among those who know what we know and receive what we receive. Every beat of our heart should be one of longing for the next moment when it will beat next to the Sacred Heart of Jesus in the time of holy Communion. I have heard it said that if the angels could be jealous of us in any way, they would have a holy jealousy of the grace of receiving holy Communion. They marvel at the love of our Savior who "commingles" himself with us, the lowest of his rational creatures, in such an intimate way. "Blessed are those who are invited to the marriage supper of the Lamb" (Rv 19:9). "The saving efficacy of the sacrifice is fully realized when the Lord's body and blood are received in Communion. The eucharistic sacrifice is intrinsically directed to the inward union of the faithful with Christ through Communion; we receive the very One who offered himself for us, we receive his Body, which he gave up for us on the cross, and his Blood, which he 'poured out for many for the forgiveness of sins' (Mt 26:28)."[99] All the prophets of the

Old Testament, such as Moses and Isaiah; all of the kings, such as David and Solomon; all of the holy women, such as Judith and Esther—even Saint John the Baptist, the greatest of all the prophets—did not experience the sublime mystery of consuming the body, blood, soul, and divinity of the Messiah in holy Communion. They must marvel at the fulfillment of what the eating of the paschal lamb signified and at the intimacy Christ desires to have with his people. "For what great nation is there that has a god so near to it as the Lord our God is to us . . . ?" (Dt 4:7). (Unfortunately, we can only wonder if they also marvel at the indifference, the lack of preparation, and the lack of thanksgiving that too often surrounds the reception of holy Communion.) A seraphim, using tongs, took a burning coal from the altar and touched it to the lips of Isaiah, taking away his guilt and sin.[100] What was a vision for Isaiah is our reality, when the burning coal of the Blessed Sacrament comes to us from the altar, and

---

[99] Pope John Paul II, *Ecclesia De Eucharistia*, § 16.

[100] "Then flew one of the seraphim to me, having in his hand a burning coal which he had taken with tongs from the altar. And he touched my mouth, and said: 'Behold, this has touched your lips; your guilt is taken away, and your sin forgiven'" (Is 6:6-7).

not only touches our lips but also is wholly consumed by us. Not even Saint Joseph had the grace that we have. Do we ponder this enough? Do we truly realize how loved and blessed we are by God to live in the time of the Eucharist, to have received the gift of eucharistic faith, and to receive within us the One before whom all of heaven falls prostrate? God's particular love for us is fully manifest in the moment of holy Communion when he has given himself not only *for* us but also *to* us completely.

The Mass is not what we do for God, but rather what God the Son has done for us. And so when Bartimaeus draws close to Christ, the Lord does not say, "What will you do for me?" but, "What do you want me to do for you?" The response of Bartimaeus is, in a spiritual and eschatological sense, a prayer for salvation. "Master, that I may see." In heaven we will receive the beatific vision, which will be the cause of our eternal ecstasy. We will see God as he truly is when we behold the divine essence. Therefore, when we come to Mass, our prayer should be the prayer of Bartimaeus. We go to Mass in order to ask our merciful Lord for the eternal vision. Then, by eating his flesh and drinking his blood, he will raise us up on the last day, the day without night, the eternal day. The Mass is Christ's prayer to the Father, and he allows us to participate in that prayer. Through the sacrifice of Christ, he appeases divine justice and obtains mercy for us. Our salvation comes through the passion and death of our Savior.

The conversation between Bartimaeus and Christ is also a beautiful image of the Liturgy of the Word. Whereas before, Jesus was not speaking directly to Bartimaeus, now he is. In the Liturgy of the Word, most especially in the proclamation of the Gospel, it is truly Jesus who speaks to us directly.[101] "And Jesus said to him, 'What do you want me to do for you?' And the blind man said to him, 'Master, let me receive my sight'" (Mk 10:51). What Bartimaeus asks for represents a soul that is well disposed to receive the graces given us through the Mass. He acknowledged the humanity of Christ when he called him "Son of David," but now he called him "Master" or "Rabboni," perceiving the hidden divinity. He asks of this man something only God can do. Upon arriving at the feet of Jesus, Bartimaeus, exercising his faith, asks for

---

[101] "Even more, it must be said that Christ himself 'is present in his word, since it is he who speaks when scripture is read in Church.'" Pope Benedict XVI, *Verbum Domini*, § 52.1.

what he would never before have thought possible. He asks for healing. The root word of *salvation* means "healing," and so salvation is the healing of our souls, strengthening them with the divine life and assistance until we reach the vision of God, when our salvation will be complete. This is what we should be seeking when we come to the feet of Jesus at the Mass.

It is interesting to note that in the other gospel accounts it says that Jesus touched Bartimaeus in order to heal him, whereas in this account of Mark, it only mentions Jesus speaking to Bartimaeus, telling him that he has been healed because of his faith. This only further helps the ties we are making here to the Mass. It is through the Mass, the graces of the cross made present to us, that we receive salvation. Christ's word and touch are what bring us healing—both scripture and Communion.

The Mode of the Receiver

As stated above, the amount that we benefit personally from the Mass depends upon our preparation for the Mass and our thanksgiving after. The principle that "everything is received according to the mode of the receiver" applies here.[102] We receive according to our capacity to receive. This is true of heaven, where our enjoyment and delight will be in proportion to how much we have loved in this life. Those who love more will be closest to God, which is why there is no creature higher than Mary. This principle also applies to our participation at Mass, where we receive grace and benefit according to the amount we love Jesus. Love is never abstract or purely intellectual, love is active. It is not enough to say we love Jesus; it must be manifest in our actions. This is why we turn first to Our Lady, the creature who loves him the most, and we ask her to teach us to love him. Mary then turns our hearts to love her Son where he is, not to just love the idea of him. We must love his life within us by grace, and we must fear losing sanctifying grace through mortal sin above all things. We must love him in the scriptures through our daily seeking of understanding in meditation and contemplation. Above all, we must love him where he is truly, really, and substantially present in the Blessed Sacrament. "To eat worthily of this heavenly bread, we must be free from mortal sin, or at least be washed from it by the blood of

---

[102] "Quidquid recipitur ad modum recipientis recipitur." Cf. Summa Theologiae, 1a, q. 75, a. 5; 3a, q. 5.

the Lamb in the sacrament of penance. One should also be free from an actual affection for any venial sin to receive Communion with greater effects."[103] "Just as the adoration of the Eucharist prepares for, accompanies, and follows the Liturgy of the Eucharist, so too prayerful reading, personal and communal, prepares for, accompanies, and deepens what the Church celebrates when she proclaims the Word in a liturgical setting."[104] This is the proximate preparation for Mass that is vitally important. Even more essential, though, is our immediate preparation for Mass and Communion, which should begin before Mass and last up to the moment we receive Jesus in the Blessed Sacrament.

Immediate preparation for Mass is the process by which, through prayer and silence, we prepare to receive the Word himself through the Liturgy of the Word and the Liturgy of the Eucharist. In order to be filled with heavenly things, we must be emptied from earthly things. If a priest is distracted during Mass, very often it is because there was never a moment of silence and prayer

[103] Thomas Crean, *The Mass and the Saints* (San Francisco: Ignatius Press, 2009), 188.

[104] Pope Benedict XVI, *Verbum Domini*, § 86.3.

before he processed out from the sacristy. Sacristies have all too often become noisy places, devoid of prayer and sacred silence, where idle conversations and useless talk drown out the voice of the Shepherd. The devil lurks in the sacristy, in order to steal recollection from the souls of priests before they step out onto the altar, and to distract them once they return after Mass from the presence of Jesus Christ who abides in them through holy Communion. No fruit will ever come from any decisions, planning, or conversations that steal from the time of preparation for Mass or thanksgiving after. For laity and religious, the preparation for Mass should also not be broken by idle talk. Certain conversations cannot be avoided for the likes of parents and families, etc., when getting ready and traveling to Mass, but too often churches have lost the gift of sacred silence. People often talk in churches as they would in a shopping mall. The Mass is a time for unity with each other that surpasses socializing. The way in which we serve our neighbor and the world at Mass is through full, active participation. This means that our minds and hearts are fixed on Christ Jesus and his sacrifice. Everything else should be set aside, including the wide array of various ministries and activities, if it keeps us from recollection on Christ and his activity at the Mass. This is portrayed beautifully by Bartimaeus when he throws aside his mantle. He rejects all earthly comfort and consolation, throws away attachments, and fixes all his focus on drawing closer to the presence of Jesus. He does this in faith, represented by the fact that he is still blind and yet walks toward Christ. Our walk of faith and hope is also a walk in darkness. "Now faith is the assurance of things hoped for, the conviction of things not seen" (Heb 11:1). Our hearts should be fixed on the person of Christ in the Blessed Sacrament, and on the sublime moment when he will come to us and abide in us through holy Communion. With that moment in mind, we empty ourselves of everything else, so as to give the eucharistic King the throne of our minds and hearts. If we are too distracted in our preparation, our attachments and other relationships will keep us from recollecting ourselves around the King who dwells within us in Communion. He will be within our body, but our minds and hearts will be concerned with lesser things. The Lord will say of us, "This people draw near with their mouth and honor me with their lips, while their hearts are far from me" (Is

29:13). We will be like the city of Bethlehem when it came time for the Lord to be born.[105] Bethlehem means "house of bread," which is what we are blessed to be when we receive "the living bread which came down from heaven" (Jn 6:51). Man is defined as a rational animal. Thus the inn of Bethlehem represents our intellect and reason, and yet we relegate the Lord to the stable where the animals are kept, which represents our body and the lower animal part of our nature. This is what happens when we do not welcome Christ into our minds and hearts when the time comes for him to be born in us in holy Communion. "He came to his own home, and his own people received him not" (Jn 1:11).

The Moment of Holy Communion

One holy Communion is sufficient to completely sanctify us, and yet we limit its effects because of our poor

---

[105] "And Joseph also went up from Galilee, from the city of Nazareth, to Judea, to the city of David, which is called Bethlehem, because he was of the house and lineage of David, to be enrolled with Mary, his betrothed, who was with child. And while they were there, the time came for her to be delivered. And she gave birth to her first-born son and wrapped him in swaddling cloths, and laid him in a manger, because there was no place for them in the inn" (Lk 2:4-7).

dispositions when we receive. The greatest problem in the world today is the indifference and sacrilege that surrounds the Blessed Sacrament and holy Communion. We limit the sanctifying effects of holy Communion in our lives because of our lack of faith, preparation, and thanksgiving. Tolkien wrote to his son, who was losing his faith, offering the following remedy: "The only cure for sagging of fainting faith is Communion. Though always itself perfect and complete and inviolate, the Blessed Sacrament does not operate completely and once for all in any of us. Like the act of faith it must be continuous and grow by exercise. Frequency is of the highest effect. Seven times a week is more nourishing than seven times at intervals."[106] Blessed Imelda, the patroness of first holy Communions, could not understand how someone could receive the Lord in the Eucharist and not die of love. She went at the age of nine to live with the Dominican sisters, and her love for the eucharistic King was evident to all. She burned with intense desire to receive Jesus. One year before she would have been of age to receive first holy Communion, which

---

[106] J. R. R. Tolkien, *The Letters of J.R.R. Tolkien: A Selection*, Kindle edition, loc. 7210-7212.

was twelve at that time, on the feast of the Ascension, Blessed Imelda was praying after Mass in front of the tabernacle. Still too young to receive holy Communion, she was communing with the Lord by drawing close to his presence. One of the sisters noticed a host hovering above Imelda, who was lost in deep prayer. They called a priest, who came and, seeing such an obvious sign of Christ's desire for Communion with this pure little soul, gave Blessed Imelda the eucharistic King. At the instant of holy Communion, when the Sacred Heart filled her heart, she died from love and entered eternity. "Holy Communion augments our union with Christ. The principal fruit of receiving the Eucharist in holy Communion is an intimate union with Christ Jesus."[107] The effectiveness of holy Communion should also not be gauged by our feelings, but by faith. Even if we don't necessarily feel the consolation of his presence, we welcome the Lord in faith, knowing that he is working within us. This is the principle we see in Bartimaeus: it is through the touch of Jesus—representing the moment of holy Communion, where we have contact with his sacred

---

[107] *Catechism of the Catholic Church*, 1391.

flesh—and Bartimaeus's own faith, which draws healing from Christ.[108] "The Eucharist truly acts within us to transform us, almost without our knowing it—as bread and wine, human nourishment, strengthens all our body and blood without our being aware of it. By his contact and the grace he leaves in us, Christ gives us moral health and creates for us another soul. It is not in vain that we lean for a moment upon his heart and confide to him our burden of suffering, weakness, and anguish."[109]

Thanksgiving

The Eucharist, and our relationship with the eucharistic Lord, is the gauge of our spiritual life. Every spirituality is drawn out and proven in the fire of the Eucharist. The lack of thanksgiving after holy Communion is the sign of a fundamental lack in authentic spirituality. All of the preparation for Mass and Communion amounts to little if we do not make a thanksgiving after Mass, spending some time gratefully enjoying the presence of Jesus and drawing from him all of the graces needed for our

[108] Mt 20:34 and Mk 10:52.

[109] Elisabeth Leseur, *Secret Diary of Elisabeth Leseur*, Kindle edition, loc 2603-2606.

sanctification. A spirituality that does not have the Eucharist as its goal and treasure is one that subtly desires something else besides Christ. "O how many of us might simplify our spiritual lives and so make great progress if we would only look to the Blessed Sacrament, to our feelings and conduct toward it, and its impression upon us, as the index of our spiritual condition!"[110] Bartimaeus is again a model for us when, after he has received his healing and is free to go his way, he chooses instead to linger in the presence of Christ. He receives sight, which is for us the moment when we receive the One who sees the Father; and then like Bartimaeus we should choose to linger and abide with Jesus. If Bartimaeus had gone his own way and not remained with Christ, then his healing would have been of no spiritual benefit to him. He would have returned to his own life without the encounter with Jesus having had its fully desired effect. To claim love for Christ, but then not abide with him when he is present within us after holy Communion, is evidence of either a lack of understanding, or lack of belief, in the doctrine of the Real Presence; or in the worst case, simply

---

[110] Father Frederick Faber, *The Blessed Sacrament* (TAN Books, 2015), Kindle edition, loc. 619-621.

indifference. To *abide* means, as we mentioned above, to "linger in the presence of." Saint Mary Magdalene de' Pazzi said, "The minutes that follow Communion are the most precious we have in our lives."[111] They are the most precious because in no other moment is the Lord as close to us as he is in the time after Communion. This presence lasts for fifteen to twenty minutes after we have received Jesus in the Eucharist. These minutes must become the very center of our lives. They must become our waking thought, and the last thing we think of before falling asleep. Every activity, every relationship, every desire should be ordered toward these minutes of holy Communion during which we experience heaven on earth. Saint Teresa of Avila devotes an entire chapter to this in *The Way of Perfection* where she begs her sisters to remember that "until the accidents of bread have been consumed by our natural heat, the good Jesus is with us and we should [not lose so good an opportunity but should] come to him. If, while he went about in the world, the sick were healed merely by touching his

---

[111] Stefano M. Manelli, *Jesus, Our Eucharistic Love: Eucharistic Life Exemplified by the Saints* (New Bedford, MA: Franciscan Friars of the Immaculate, 2008, ©1996), 45.

clothes, how can we doubt that he will work miracles when he is within us, if we have faith, or that he will give us what we ask of him since he is in our house? His majesty is not wont to offer us too little payment for his lodging if we treat him well."[112] "Delight to remain with him; do not lose such an excellent time for talking with him as the hour after Communion. Remember that this is a very profitable hour for the soul; if you spend it in the company of the good Jesus, you are doing him a great service. Be very careful, then, daughters, not to lose it."[113] As Flannery O'Connor said, the Eucharist "is the center of existence for me; all the rest of life is expendable." When a friar confessed not making his thanksgiving because some ministry impeded him, Saint Padre Pio "became stern and he said firmly, 'Let us see to it that our being unable is not just being unwilling. I always have to make my thanksgiving; otherwise I pay dearly.'"[114]

---

[112] Saint Teresa of Avila, *The Way of Perfection by Saint Teresa of Avila* (Ignacio Hills Press, 2009), Kindle edition, 106.

[113] Ibid., 107.

[114] Stefano M. Manelli, *Jesus, Our Eucharistic Love: Eucharistic Life Exemplified by the Saints*, 47.

Stay with Me, Lord

(Prayer of St. Pio of Pietrelcina after Holy Communion)

Stay with me, Lord, for it is necessary to have

You present so that I do not forget you.

You know how easily I abandon you.

Stay with me, Lord, because I am weak

and I need your strength, that I may not fall so often.

Stay with me, Lord, for you are my life,

and without you, I am without fervor.

Stay with me, Lord, for you are my light,

and without you, I am in darkness.

Stay with me, Lord, to show me your will.

Stay with me, Lord, so that I hear your voice and follow you.

Stay with me, Lord, for I desire to love you

very much, and always be in your company.

Stay with me, Lord, if you wish me to be faithful to you.

Stay with me, Lord, for as poor as my soul is,

I want it to be a place of consolation for you, a nest of love.

Stay with me, Jesus, for it is getting late and the day is coming to

a close, and life passes; death, judgment, eternity approaches.

It is necessary to renew my strength,

so that I will not stop along the way and for that, I need you.

It is getting late and death approaches,

I fear the darkness, the temptations,

the dryness, the cross, the sorrows.

O how I need you, my Jesus, in this night of exile!

Stay with me tonight, Jesus,

in life with all its dangers. I need you.

Let me recognize you as your disciples did

at the breaking of the bread, so that the eucharistic Communion

be the light which disperses the darkness,

the force which sustains me, the unique joy of my heart.

Stay with me, Lord, because at the hour of my death,

I want to remain united to you, if not by communion,

at least by grace and love.

Stay with me, Jesus, I do not ask for divine consolation,

because I do not merit it, but the gift of your presence,

oh yes, I ask this of you!

Stay with me, Lord, for it is you alone I look for,

Your love, your grace, your will, your heart, your Spirit,

because I love you and ask no other reward

but to love you more and more.

With a firm love, I will love you with all my heart while on earth and continue to love you perfectly during all eternity. Amen."

CONCLUSION:
A TRULY NEW AND EUCHARISTIC
EVANGELIZATION

————————— • —————————

The purpose of these five principles is to give a practical way in which we can live our lives *from* and *for* Jesus Christ in the Eucharist. The consequences of following them, depending on the love with which they are applied and lived, will be the perfection of our prayer, our spiritual lives, and our apostolates and mission. "The mode of Christ's presence under the eucharistic species is unique. It raises the Eucharist above all the sacraments as 'the perfection of the spiritual life and the end to which all the sacraments tend.'"[115]

---

[115] *Catechism of the Catholic Church*, revised ed. (London: Burns

There is a lot of talk within Catholic circles about the new evangelization, and many efforts have been started in order to carry out this much-needed mission. These efforts have succeeded to various degrees, depending upon the extent and depth of their relationship to the Eucharist.[116] "The Eucharist is the source and summit of the life and mission of the Church."[117] Any work or mission that does not have the Eucharist as its source will not have sufficient power to accomplish anything meaningful or truly lasting. Any work that does not have the Eucharist as its summit and goal is misdirected. "The

& Oates, 2011), 1374.

[116] "Join me in asking Jesus Christ the Lord, who died for our sins and rose for our salvation, that as a result of this eucharistic congress the whole Church may be *strengthened for the new evangelization which the whole world needs:* new, also because of its explicit and deep reference to the Eucharist as the center and source of Christian life, as the seed and requisite of fellowship, justice, and service to all humanity, starting with those who are most needy in body and in spirit. Evangelization *through* the Eucharist, *in* the Eucharist, and *from* the Eucharist: these are three inseparable aspects of how the Church lives the mystery of Christ and fulfills her mission of communicating it to all people." Pope John Paul II, *We Adore God Present Among Us*, https://www.ewtn.com/library/PAPALDOC/JP2EUCAD.HTM, accessed 10 June 2017.

[117] Synod of Bishops, XI Ordinary General Assembly, The Eucharist: Source and Summit of the Life and Mission of the Church *Instrumentum Laboris* (7 July 2005).

efficacy of an apostolate almost invariably corresponds to the degree of eucharistic life acquired by a soul. Indeed, the sure sign of a successful apostolate is when it makes souls thirst for frequent and fruitful participation in the divine banquet. And this result will never be obtained except in proportion as the apostle himself really makes Jesus in the Blessed Sacrament the source and center of his life."[118] "It is impossible to meditate upon the consequences of the dogma of the Real Presence, of the sacrifice of the altar, and of Communion without being led to the conclusion that Our Lord wanted to institute this sacrament in order to make it the center of all action, of all loyal idealism, of every apostolate that could be of any real use to the Church. If our whole redemption gravitates about Calvary, all the graces of the mystery flow down upon us from the altar. And the gospel worker who does not draw all his life from the altar utters only a word that is dead, a word that cannot save souls, because it comes from a heart that is not sufficiently steeped in the precious Blood."[119]

---

[118] Chautard, *Soul of the Apostolate*, Kindle edition, 189.

[119] Ibid., 187.

We cannot evangelize effectively until we have been evangelized. Successful evangelization is not measured in terms of quantity but quality. Have we truly brought people to know Christ, to love Christ, to receive sanctifying grace through the sacraments and eventually be united to him in holy Communion? "Missionary activity does not fully attain its objective until it gathers ecclesial communities to proclaim their faith in the celebration of the Eucharist."[120] Authentic renewal in the Church is measured by intensity of love for the Eucharist.[121] Once we have experienced the overwhelming love of Christ in the Blessed Sacrament, this love becomes the compelling force that drives effective evangelization. We grow in the desire to make Jesus known and loved in the Blessed Sacrament, and we increasingly share in the love that he has for souls. Evangelization, on the part of the apostles, began when they were called by Christ to follow

---

[120] Pope John Paul II, *L' Osservatore Romano*, Audience with the Pontifical Committee for Eucharistic Congresses and the National Delegates (7 November 1991).

[121] "The encouragement and the deepening of eucharistic worship are proofs of that authentic renewal which the council set itself as an aim and of which they are the central point." Pope John Paul II, Letter on the Mystery and Worship of the Eucharist *Dominicae Cenae* (24 February 1980), § 3.

him. They spent years in his presence, listening to his teachings, witnessing his miracles, and absorbing his life. The culmination of their formation, before being sent out into the world, took place in the upper room where the Eucharist was instituted, united in prolonged hours of prayer with Mary, awaiting the outpouring of the Holy Spirit and power from on high. It would be presumptuous to attempt any other preparation for evangelization than this. Why would we build another model of formation when the one given us by Christ is so perfect, so beautiful, and so effective? Our own formation for evangelization should involve sufficient time in his eucharistic presence and loving attention and meditation upon the mysteries of his life in the gospels. It should involve long hours of prayer, united with Mary, in the presence of the Blessed Sacrament, awaiting true inspiration and power for our apostolates and evangelization.

To rush into evangelization without being centered on the eucharistic Christ, and without a deep interior life, is to forget that he is God, and we are not. If we do not abide in him, we can do nothing (cf. John 15:5). To begin without being firmly established in Christ is to place ourselves as the source of grace for evangelization. "Now for a man, in his practical conduct, to go about his active works as if Jesus were not his one and only life principle, is what Cardinal Mermillod has called the 'heresy of good works.' He uses this expression to stigmatize the apostle who so far forgets himself as to overlook his secondary and subordinate role, and look only to his own personal activity and talents as a basis for apostolic success. Is this not, in practice, a denial of a great part of the tract on grace? This conclusion is one that appalls us, at first sight. And yet a little thought will show us that it is only too true. Heresy in good works! Feverish activity taking the place of God; grace ignored; human pride trying to thrust Jesus from his throne; supernatural life, the power of prayer, the economy of our redemption relegated, at least in practice, to the realm of pure theory: all this portrays no merely imaginary situation, but one which the diagnosis of souls shows to be very common though in various degrees, in this age of naturalism, when men judge, above all, by appearances, and act as though success were primarily a matter of skillful organization."[122]

---

[122] Chautard, *Soul of the Apostolate*, Kindle edition, 11-12.

Prayer is not just one thing among many that is necessary for evangelization; rather, prayer and grace are primary. The interior life comes first; everything else follows after. All too often prayer and conversation with God are no longer what guides parish life and mission. Time talking with God has been supplanted with hours of meetings, where conclusions are drawn from personal preferences and opinions. Meetings, obsessive activity, and excessive talking give the illusion of accomplishing something good yet can be a distraction from what the Lord has willed for us. They can also become an excuse for not submitting ourselves to the uncomfortable purifications necessary in the interior life, those brought about by faithful, loving, and silent daily prayer. I met someone who was part of a group whose mission was to care for the poor; this person was rightly frustrated that the group spent literally hours every week in meetings, yet only thirty minutes at most with those in need, and not even one minute in prayer together. Planning and organization are important, but not when they become an end in themselves. They should never be a replacement for prayer and discernment. We should spend more time praying for effective evangelization than talking about it.

We must first be evangelized before we begin evangelizing others. We should allow the Good News to wash over us and fill us with the joy of knowing Christ. We have to carry from our time in eucharistic adoration and holy Communion the lingering aroma of Christ out into in the world. Time spent in prayerful, loving meditation on scripture will cause our hearts to burn within us, rendering us able to set the world ablaze.[123]

The process by which Bartimaeus is healed from blindness is a beautiful image of the simplicity of what is required for effective evangelization. There are two things he hears that change his life forever and lead him to an intimate encounter with the living God: he hears that Jesus is present, and he hears the words of Christ communicated to him by souls who have themselves spent time in the presence of Jesus and have listened to his words. This is enough to make Bartimaeus leave everything and follow Christ. We can have a tendency to overcomplicate things. Jesus is so beautiful; he is the deep desire of every human heart. We have only to tell people

---

[123] "They said to each other, 'Did not our hearts burn within us while he talked to us on the road, while he opened to us the scriptures?'" (Lk 24:32).

where he is. If we but raise him up, he will draw all mankind to himself.[124] There is nothing as compelling and powerful as the presence of Christ and a line from holy scripture to change a hardened heart. It was often one simple line from scripture that began the vocation of some of the most extraordinary saints. Souls are thirsting for Christ, and we have only to bring them his grace, his Mother, his word, and himself in the Blessed Sacrament.

Thy kingdom come, Lord Jesus!

---

[124] "And I, when I am lifted up from the earth, will draw all men to myself" (Jn 12:32).

BIBLIOGRAPHY

————————•————————

Aquinas, Thomas. *Catena Aurea: Commentary on the Four Gospels*, Vol. 1-4. London, John Henry Parker: Oxford, 2011. Kindle edition.

Benedict XVI. Angelus, 18 September 2005.

Benedict XVI. Encyclical on Christian Hope *Spe Salvi*, 30 November 2007.

Benedict XVI. Post-Synodal Apostolic Exhortation on the Word of God in the Life   and   Mission   of   the Church *Verbum Domini*, 30 September 2010.

Benedict XVI. Post-Synodal Apostolic Exhortation on the Eucharist as the Source and Summit of the Church's Life and Mission *Sacramentum Caritatis*, 22 February 2007.

Benedict XVI. *Jesus of Nazareth: From the Baptism in the Jordan to the Transfiguration.* New York: Doubleday, 2007.

Bougaud, Emile. *Revelations of the Sacred Heart to Blessed Margaret Mary and the History of Her Life.* New York: Benziger Brothers, 1890. Kindle edition.

Catechism of the Catholic Church, revised ed. London: Burns & Oates, 2011.

Chautard, Dom Jean-Baptiste. *Soul of the Apostolate.* TAN Books, 1977. Kindle edition.

Congregation for Divine Worship and the Discipline of the Sacraments on Certain Matters to be Observed or To Be Avoided Regarding the Most Holy Eucharist *Redemptionis Sacramentum*, 23 April 2004.

Crean, Thomas. *The Mass and the Saints*. San Francisco: Ignatius Press, 2009.

Dante, Alighieri. *The Inferno*. Edited and translated by Anthony M. Esolen and Gustave Doré. The Modern Library Classics. New York: Modern Library, 2005.

Eudes, Jean. *The Admirable Heart of Mary*. Translated by Ruth Hauser. Fort Erie, Ont.: Immaculate Heart of Mary, 2007.

Evert, Jason. *Saint John Paul the Great: His Five Loves*. Lakewood, CO: Totus Tuus Press, 2014. Kindle edition.

Faber, Father Frederick. *The Blessed Sacrament*. TAN Books, 2015. Kindle edition.

Fabre, Father Frederick. *The Foot of the Cross with Mary: or The Sorrows of Mary*. KIC, 2015. Kindle edition.

Francis of Sales. *Introduction to the Devout Life — Enhanced Version*, Christian Classics Ethereal Library, 2009.

Garrigou-Lagrange, Rev. Reginald, OP. *The Mother of the Saviour and Our Interior Life.* Catholic Way Publishing, 2013.

Gregory the Great. *Morals on the Book of Job.* Edited by Paul A Boer, Sr. London: Veritatis Splendor Publications, 2012. Kindle edition.

Hahn, Scott. *Consuming the Word: The New Testament and the Eucharist in the Early Church.* New York: The Doubleday Religious Publishing Group, 2013. Kindle edition.

John of the Cross. *The Collected Works of St. John of the Cross.* 2d ed. ICS Publications. Washington, D. C.: Institute of Carmelite Studies, 1979.

John Paul II, Homily given in Seville on the 12 June 1993, *We Adore God Present Among Us,* https://www.ewtn.com/library/PAPALDOC/JP2EUCA D.HTM, accessed 10 June 2017.

John Paul II. *L' Osservatore Romano*, Audience with the Pontifical Committee for Eucharistic Congresses and the National Delegates, 7 November 1991.

John Paul II. Letter to the Bishop of Liege on the 750th Anniversary of the feast of Corpus Christi (28 May 1996), at https://catholicsaints.info/pope-john-paul-ii-letter-on-the-750th-anniversary-of-the-feast-of-corpus-christi-28-may-1996/. accessed 11 June 2017.

John Paul II. Letter on the Mystery and Worship of the Eucharist *Dominicae Cenae*, 24 February 1980.

John Paul II. Encyclical on the Eucharist in its Relationship to the Church *Ecclesia de Eucharistia*, 17 April 2003.

John Paul II. Encyclical on the Splendor of Truth *Veritatis Splendor*, 6 August 1993.

Leseur, Elisabeth. *Secret Diary of Elisabeth Leseur*. Manchester, New Hampshire: Sophia Institute Press, 2012. Kindle edition.

Louis Marie de Montfort. *The Secret of the Rosary.* 2013. Kindle edition.

Manelli, Stefano M. Jesus. *Our Eucharistic Love: Eucharistic Life Exemplified by the Saints.* New Bedford, MA: Franciscan Friars of the Immaculate, 2008, ©1996.

Marmion, Columba. *Our Way and Our Life: Christ in His Mysteries,* abridged ed. Tacoma, WA: Angelico Press, 2013. Kindle edition.

Martínez, Luis M., *The Sanctifier* (2nd ed.). Boston, MA: Pauline Books & Media, 2003.

Paul VI. Dogmatic Constitution on the Church *Lumen Gentium,* 21 November 1964.

Raymond of Capua. *The Life of St. Catherine of Siena: The Classic on Her Life and Accomplishments as Recorded by Her Spiritual Director.* Charlotte, North Carolina: TAN Books, 2011. Kindle edition.

Sheen, Fulton. *The Eucharist God Among Us*. Retreat on the Priesthood 2, Audio, from FultonSheen.com. Catholic MP3 Vault, 2011.

Teresa of Avila. *The Way of Perfection by Saint Teresa of Avila*. Ignacio Hills Press, 2009. Kindle edition.

Stein, Edith. *Essays on Woman*. 2nd ed. Edited by L. Gelber and Romaeus Leuven. Washington, D. C.: ICS Publications, 1996. Kindle edition.

Synod of Bishops. XI Ordinary General Assembly. The Eucharist: Source and Summit of the Life and Mission of the Church *Instrumentum Laboris*, 7 July 2005.

Tolkien, J. R. R. *The Letters of J. R. R. Tolkien: A Selection*. Edited by Humphrey Carpenter and Christopher Tolkien. HarperCollins, 2015. Kindle edition.

ABOUT THE AUTHOR

Father Barry Braum is a member of the Missionaries of the Most Holy Eucharist. After being ordained a priest on June 28, 2015, by Bishop Dominique Rey in France, he spent two years serving at the Eucharistic Retreat Center in the Seminary of the Immaculate Conception, Long Island. He is currently pursuing an STL in Dogmatic theology at the Angelicum in Rome.

CPSIA information can be obtained
at www.ICGtesting.com
Printed in the USA
FSHW010900170219
55734FS